JAMESTOWN'S STORY

Act One of
the American Dream

PARKE ROUSE, JR.

Compiled and Edited

by Wilford Kale

To commemorate the 400th Anniversary of
Jamestown, Virginia

Dietz Press
Richmond, Virginia

JAMESTOWN'S STORY

Act One *of the* American Dream

PARKE ROUSE, JR.

❧ ❧ ❧ ❧

Compiled and Edited by

Wilford Kale

To commemorate the 400th Anniversary of

Jamestown, Virginia

For my two sons, Walker and Carter Kale —
adventurers in their own time.

Copyright © 2006 Parke Shepherd Rouse III, Sarah Rouse Sheehan, and Marshall Rouse McClure

Designed by Marshall Rouse McClure

Printed in the United States

2008 Second printing

Chapters 1, 7, 14, 15, 23, 25, 26, 27, 28, 29, 30, and 31
Copyright © Daily Press, Newport News, Virginia, A Tribune Publishing Company

Prologue and Chapters 12, 16, 18, and 21 from *Planters and Pioneers—Life in Colonial Virginia*,
Hastings House Publishers, New York, Copyright © 1968 Parke Rouse, Jr.

Chapters 2, 3, 10, 13 and part of 9 from *Virginia—The English Heritage in America*,
Hastings House Publishers, New York, Copyright © 1966 by Parke Rouse, Jr.

Chapters 4, 5, 6, 8, 11, 17, 20, and part of 19, from *The Iron Worker*, Copyright © Lynchburg
Foundry Company, now owned by Intermet Corporation of Troy, Michigan

Chapters 22, 24, 32, and part of 19 from *The James—Where A Nation Began*,
The Dietz Press, Copyright © 1990 Parke Rouse, Jr.

Chapter 33 from the Jamestown Festival Official Program, 1957

Chapter 34 from *Remembering Williamsburg—A Sentimental Journey through Three Centuries*,
The Dietz Press, Copyright © 1989 Parke Rouse, Jr.

Published by
Dietz Press
Richmond, Virginia

Softbound
ISBN: 0-87517-130-3
LCN: 2005928842

Hardbound
ISBN: 0-87517-132-X
LCN: 2005934906

Table of Contents ❧

PART I ❧ Jamestown in the Beginning

PART II ❦ Jamestown Vignettes

Foreword ❧

I n 1957, the name Parke Shepherd Rouse, Jr. was synonymous with Jamestown, the site of Virginia's and the nation's commemoration of the 350th anniversary of the first permanent English settlement in the New World.

Parke Rouse knew and loved Jamestown and its colorful history. Therefore, his selection as director of the state's commemorative celebration was a logical connective.

From 1954, when he was first appointed, until 1980, when he retired, Parke worked at Jamestown Foundation's Festival Park (the scene of Virginia's commemoration in 1957 and now called the Jamestown Settlement). The Jamestown Foundation became the Jamestown-Yorktown Foundation, one of the state's more unusual agencies, operating two tourist-oriented facilities. In addition, from 1974 until 1980, he served as executive director of the Virginia Independence Bicentennial Commission, which established three major historic interpretive/visitor centers in Alexandria, Charlottesville, and Yorktown.

But it is Jamestown for which Parke is most remembered and appreciated.

A native of Smithfield, Virginia, Parke grew up in Newport News and received his bachelor's degree in English at Washington and Lee University in 1937. He served on the reporting staffs of the *Newport News Times-Herald* and the *Richmond Times-Dispatch* newspapers prior to joining the U.S. Navy at the beginning of World War II. A naval officer, he participated in action in Sicily and Salerno and later saw duty while on the staff of Admiral Chester Nimitz in the Pacific. After the war, he returned to the *Times-Dispatch*, first on the editorial staff as writer and assistant to the newspaper's editor, Virginius Dabney, and later as the Sunday Editor.

In 1950 Parke joined the Virginia State Chamber of Commerce and in 1953 became director of publications for Colonial Williamsburg, working closely with Carlisle H. Humelsine, then Colonial Williamsburg's "on-site" director of the historical operation and later its president and chairman.

In 1954 the Commonwealth of Virginia tapped him to direct the 350th anniversary festival commemo-

Parke Rouse, Jr. with costumed interpreter John Crull at Jamestown Festival Park in the late 1960s when Rouse was executive director of the Jamestown Foundation, a state agency that operated the facility. (From the Rouse Collection, Special Collections, Earl Gregg Swem Library, College of William and Mary)

rating the English settlement in 1607 at Jamestown and to oversee the construction of Jamestown Festival Park. From that office he moved to become executive director of the state agency that operated Jamestown Festival Park, where he remained until his retirement.

For more than 15 years, Parke wrote a column for the Newport News *Daily Press* about Tidewater Virginia, the land he knew and cherished. Virginia Governor Gerald Baliles proclaimed him a Virginia Laureate for his contributions in preserving the Commonwealth's heritage.

In addition to his newspaper work, Parke's writings appeared in the *Saturday Evening Post*, the *New York Times Magazine*, *American Heritage*, *The Commonwealth* and *The Iron Worker* magazines, among others.

He also wrote more than 20 books and pamphlets. For Colonial Williamsburg he wrote *The City That Turned Back Time*, *They Gave Us Freedom*, and *The Colonial Printer*. His other books included *Virginia—The English Heritage in America*; *Planters and Pioneers: Life in Colonial Virginia*; *Below the James Lies Dixie*; *Endless Harbor—The Story of Newport News*; *James Blair of Virginia*; *Roll, Chesapeake, Roll—Chronicles of the Great Bay*; *The Great Wagon Road—From Philadelphia to the South*; *Cows on the Campus—Williamsburg in Bygone Days*; *A House for a President—250 Years on the Campus of the College of William and Mary*; *The Timber Tycoons—The Camp Families of Virginia and Florida and Their Empire, 1887–1987*; *The James—Where a Nation Began*; *Remembering Williamsburg—A Sentimental Journey through Three Centuries*; *Along Virginia's Golden Shores—Glimpses of Tidewater Life*; *The Good Old Days in Hampton and Newport News*; and *We Happy WASPs—Virginia in the Days of Jim Crow and Harry Byrd*.

At his death in 1997, Parke was hailed as a widely respected historian of his native Commonwealth, especially the Tidewater area that he loved. If there was a question on Newport News, Jamestown, or Williamsburg history, Parke was the first person to be consulted. On the rare occasion when he did not know the answer, he knew where to find it.

An obituary written by longtime Williamsburg-James City County resident and veteran editor/reporter Will Molineux of the Newport News *Daily Press*, said: "While [Rouse's] interest encompassed colonial times as well as contemporary events, he was fond of focusing on vignettes and anecdotes. He was a celebrated raconteur who

relished reciting the history that he had been taught and telling of the life experiences he remembered. For him, history was personal, but something personal that was meant to be shared.

"…While he was active in promoting the landmarks of Virginia as tourist attractions, his primary interest was in preserving the Virginia story—the notable feats of patriots and planters, of militiamen and craftsmen, of revolutionaries and rebels, of college professors and clergymen."

Parke Rouse, Jr. (right) and the Spanish ambassador examine a document related to Jamestown. (From the Jamestown-Yorktown Foundation)

As the 400th anniversary of the Jamestown settlement approached it occurred to Parke's family and friends that selections from his newspaper columns, books and various other writings on Jamestown could be compiled to chronicle the dramatic story of the beginning of English America. With the help and encouragement of his widow, Betsy Gayle Rouse, who died in 2002, and later his children—Sarah, Marshall, and Shepherd—this project came together in a form that models Parke's later published works. We think he would have approved.

Wilford Kale
September, 2005

Prologue ⚜

It was late afternoon on May 13, 1607. Three sailing ships wind slowly up the James River in Virginia. The smallest ship pushes ahead to test the depth, while her crew and passengers scan the shore for a suitable mooring. Then the captain of the lead ship sights a peninsula jutting into the channel and noses his ship toward its shore, signaling the others to follow.

By such means the *Discovery* led the *Susan Constant* and *Godspeed* to Virginia 400 years ago. In the unearthly glow of sunset, they tied their bows to overhanging trees and prepared to land their 104 passengers and cargo next day. England's flag—the red cross of St. George on a white field—brightened the gloom of the pine forest.

Thus was born "King James His Towne," later known as Jamestown. Small as it was, it was to be remembered as the beginning of England overseas. Lord James Bryce, British statesman of the early twentieth century, called it one of the epic events in the life of man. It was the beginning of the American era in world history.

The securing of the beachhead was no easy achievement. Thousands of Englishmen lost their lives to establish a foothold in the swamp. Its career was the commencement of the American success story—from crude infancy to world power. The settlement of Virginia was the beginning of Act One of the American dream.

(*Editor's note*: This book tells the story of the men and women who came from the green fields of England to people that dream. It is the story of John Smith and his fruitless efforts to find gold, of John Rolfe and his timely planting of tobacco, and

The settlers arrived at Jamestown on May 13, 1607 and came ashore the next day. (From a postal card by Jamestown Amusement & Vending Co., Inc. of Norfolk for the 1907 Jamestown Exposition, courtesy of the editor)

of Governor Sir George Yeardley and his first legislative assembly in America in 1619. There is also a "miscellany" designed to expand the story of Jamestown, including efforts in 1907 and 1957 to commemorate Jamestown's settlements with festivals of state and national importance.)

But Virginia was not only the province of Englishmen. It was the land of Powhatan, "Emperor of the Western World," and his tribes on whose land the settlers began to carve out their own destiny. Virginia grew also from the sweat of thousands of Black slaves, brought in chains from Africa. Their legacy also brought rich traditions to the land. Other Europeans came through the years.

The enduring church tower of about 1690 on Jamestown Island recalls the British beginnings in Virginia. (From the Rouse Collection, Special Collections, Earl Gregg Swem Library, College of William and Mary, photo by the Newport News Daily Press*)*

Amid the toil and sweat were hardship and death. But if so many died, why did so many come?

Call it "the Virginian fever," as Ben Johnson did. Call it hope or ambition. Whatever you call it, it was man's eternal search for a better life. Like most human ventures, the migration had elements of both idealism and the desire for gain. Hemmed in by class distinctions in the old country, men like Rolfe wanted the freedom that Virginia offered. But more than that, Virginia's settlers wanted to own land, to make money, and to bring up children with hope of a bright future.

To the middle-class Englishman or Scotsman who came, the passage to Virginia seemed a ticket in a vast lottery. He had so much to gain in that boundless and abundant country. The Virginia Company investors looked for profit, too. With such vast natural wealth in Virginia, it should be easy to produce many profitable articles that England needed. Thus Virginia's was a planned economy from the beginning. Gold and silver must be sought first. Then ship's masts, ship's stores, and such new luxury articles as glass, silk, wine, and tobacco, all of which England wanted. In return for Virginia's products, of course, her settlers must take English manufactures.

So it was that tobacco became synonymous with Virginia. In fact, the honey-colored leaf soon was Virginia's economy, for lack of adequate English coinage. But the colony's dependence on one luxury export put Virginians increasingly at the mercy of the merchants of London. Around the tables of London coffee houses, a handful of tobacco buyers could set the prices for a whole year's work on all Virginia's plantations. Thus, in the building of empire, the colonists had always been at the mercy of the mother country.

Nevertheless, there was a certain freedom. This was guaranteed even more by the establishment in 1619 of the first legislative assembly in America. This self-government, begun in Jamestown's wooden church inside the palisaded fort, would grow, nurtured by the men and women who themselves were becoming Virginians. Their efforts would eventually, about 150 years later, lead to an independence never dreamed by those first colonists—a government of the people, by the people, and for the people. The United States of America.

Jamestown is the beginning of their story. ❧

Planters and Pioneers—Life in Colonial Virginia, Hastings House Publishers, New York, 1968

PART I
Jamestown in the Beginning

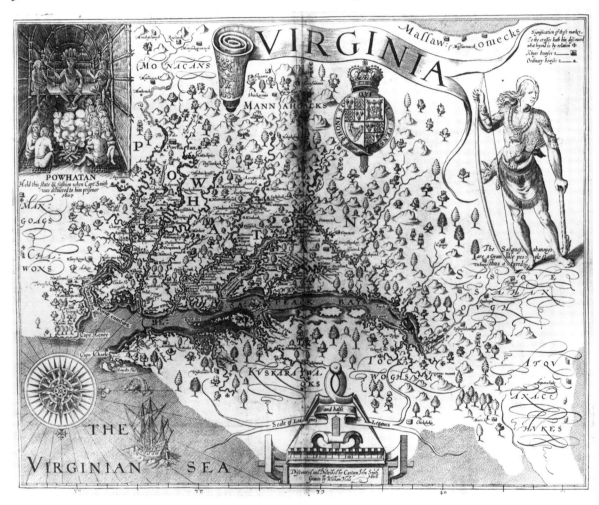

Captain John Smith's famous map of Virginia in the early seventeenth century focuses on the Chesapeake Bay and its tributaries. (From The Generall Historie of Virginia, New-England, and the Summer Isles, *[1612], courtesy the Jamestown-Yorktown Foundation)*

CHAPTER 1

The Spanish Came First

Few people realize that the Spanish attempted to colonize Tidewater Virginia well before the English landed at Jamestown in 1607. In fact, it was 37 years before the era of Captains John Smith and Christopher Newport and may have been in the same area where the English finally founded a colony.

Connecticut history scholar Dr. Charlotte Grandie blames Spain's failure in Virginia on conflict between its Jesuit missionaries and the hard-boiled Spanish soldiers. But for Spain's bungling, Virginia's coast might have been wrestled by the Spanish from Indians in the sixteenth century, as the Spaniards later won California.

Spain's Virginia adventures came in two segments—in 1525 and later in 1570. Initially, Lucas Vasquez de Ayllon was authorized by King Carlos I of Spain to settle the North American mainland. After traveling to Santo Domingo, he sailed northward to the mouth of the Chesapeake Bay in 1525. From a description by Vasquez de Ayllon, he apparently settled on the peninsula where the English located their colony some 80 years later. The Spaniards called it "Guandape," a name the Virginia Indians were still using in 1607, when the English arrived to name it Jamestown.

The Spanish had some poor luck. Their leader, Vasquez de Ayllon, died of fever, and those who succeeded him had neither the toughness nor the ability necessary to survive in the Virginia wilderness, and they went

Jesuit priests, including Father Juan Bapt: de Segura, were killed in Florida trying to convert the Indians. The Indian costume and weapons reflect the contemporary European notions. (From Societas Jesu usque ad sanguinis et vitae...*[1675])*

back to Santo Domingo. Spain did not gain a colony on the continent until 1565, when settlers came to Florida and founded St. Augustine, the oldest continuous European settlement in what is now the United States.

Two Jesuit scholars, Fathers Clifford Lewis and Albert Loomie, first revealed Spain's attempted 1570 settlement on the Virginia Peninsula in their book, *The Spanish Jesuit Mission in Virginia, 1570–1572*, published in 1953 by the University of North Carolina Press. Since then, several other scholars have dug deeper into the Madrid archives. They revive an old question: Why did powerful Spain lose its sixteenth-century primacy to Great Britain?

Scholars suggest several reasons: The weak leadership of Spain's King Philip II and the conflict between the conquistadors and missionaries.

The key figure in Spain's effort to settle the Chesapeake area was its first military governor of Florida, the cruel Don Pedro Menendez. He had brought Spain's flag to St. Augustine in 1565 with the promise to his king to clear the area of all foreigners and "heretics" and to explore the coast northward to what we now call Newfoundland.

Menendez was especially anxious to claim the Chesapeake Bay, which the Spaniards called Bahia de Santa Maria. He believed it was "the northernmost habitable area south of Newfoundland," writes Dr. Grandie in an article in the 1988 edition of the *Virginia Magazine of History and Biography*. The bay was the natural boundary between Spain's Florida claims and France's claim to what is now Canada. Alas, that led to Menendez's disappointment.

In 1565 Menendez wrote from Florida to King Philip to point out how useful the Chesapeake would be. He planned to take 250 Spanish soldiers to the bay, but instead sent 30 soldiers and two Dominican friars the next year. They returned without even disembarking, claiming a storm had driven them out to sea.

Menendez then sent a second expedition to Virginia in 1570, apparently landing near Jamestown on the James River. The 10 settlers, two of them Jesuit priests, spent a year in the midst of a severe drought. Eventually, the hungry missionaries crossed the Peninsula to the York River, where Indians killed all but one.

Dr. Grandie blames the Jesuits' failure in Virginia and elsewhere on the Atlantic coast on their intolerance of non-Spanish cultures. She blames Spain's narrow nationalism on long years of battling Islam and on pride in Spanish blood lines. In its harsh treatment of the Indians, the Spanish embodied a "belief that Spanish culture was materially and morally superior to any other," she writes.

Their Christianity, she said, was intolerant of Indians' spiritual beliefs, and the "Spanish Jesuits naturally carried this intolerance with them."

Similarly, Virginia's Powhatan Indians by 1570 had developed their own cultural identity and rejected Spain's, and later England's, culture. "Caught between the sea and the Siousan tribes who threatened them in Piedmont Virginia, Powhatan's tribesmen strongly resisted Spain's attempted Jesuit mission in 1570," the historian writes. The book by Fathers Lewis and Loomie tells the sad story of eight Jesuit missionaries and a lone Spanish boy, Alonso, who apparently landed near the mouth of College Creek, just east of Jamestown. There the Indians were suffering from a lengthy drought, but Father Juan Baptista de Segura, the Spanish leader, decided to stay anyway and sent the ship back to Florida.

The Spanish had brought an Indian interpreter, Don Luis, with them to Virginia and he was helpful initially, but later deserted them and joined the natives who surrounded the tiny Spanish group. In search of a location to build their mission, the Jesuits decided to cross the Peninsula near present-day Williamsburg and settled near Queen's Creek on the York River, not far from Kiskiak, an Indian village. They were murdered at the site a short time later, apparently with the assistance of the treacherous Don Luis.

A year after bringing the Jesuits to Virginia, a Spanish ship in 1571 sailed up the Atlantic coast from St. Augustine to deliver provisions to the Virginia mission. Arriving in the York River, the ship found Indians parading on shore "vested in cassocks and religious robes." They rescued the Spanish boy, Alonso, the lone survivor and took him back to Florida. A second Spanish rescue mission in 1572 learned that the Jesuits were dead. In revenge, the Spanish killed eight Indian hostages.

Early English historians like Richard Hakluyt left fragmentary records of several Spanish and British voyages in the Chesapeake Bay, but missed the Jesuits' effort to settle the Virginia area. Authors Lewis and Loomie searched the Spanish archives in

Jesuit missionaries settled on the James River in 1570 and crossed the Peninsula to start a mission later on the York. (From the Rouse Collection, Special Collections, Earl Gregg Swem Library, College of William and Mary, courtesy of the University of North Carolina Press)

Madrid to discover early Spanish maps of the Chesapeake and accounts written by explorers, particularly Fathers Segura and Louis de Quiros, who wrote their Jesuit superiors in Florida and in Spain.

"There are more people here than in any of the other lands I have seen so far along the coast explored," wrote Father Juan Rogel. "It seemed to me that the natives are more settled than in other regions I have been, and I am confident that should Spaniards settle here (provided they would frighten the natives that threaten harm), we could preach the Holy Gospel more easily than elsewhere."

"After the death of Spain's King Philip II in 1598," concludes Dr. Grandie, "the struggle for power between the Spanish monarchy and the Jesuit generals lessened." After Spain felt secure in Mexico, her priests moved up the Pacific coast to present-day Arizona and California. Their early missions still survive there.

Spanish Jesuit missionaries were slain in Florida by the native Indians, as this seventeenth-century engraving illustrates. This fate was similar to that of the Jesuits who attempted to settle near Jamestown in the sixteenth century. (From Societas Jesu usque ad sanguinis et vitae... *[1675])*

Spain's success on the Pacific coast was caused by its change of tactics from those in Virginia, Dr. Grandie thinks. Spain was wise in wanting to claim the Chesapeake because it could have opened a new world for them. Had Spain succeeded, neighboring Spaniards might have frustrated John Smith's 1607 settlement at Jamestown.

In that case, the Jesuits' Virginia mission of 1570 could have changed history. 🪷

Newport News Daily Press, June 1988 and

The James—Where A Nation Began, The Dietz Press, Richmond, 1990

CHAPTER 2 ❧

Raleigh and His "Lost Colony"

While the Spanish and Portuguese were exploring and settling in the Americas, the English chafed under the limitations of a second-rate power and yearned for the day when they could challenge their Iberian rivals. The last half of the sixteenth century brought rapid growth of home industry and towns to England, turning the island into a nation of shopkeepers, ambitious and independent of mind, spurring the building of merchant ships.

From the hour of her enthronement in 1558 until her death 45 years later, Queen Elizabeth inspired the exploits of a succession of sea captains and explorers who advanced England on land and sea. Taking advantage of the temporary peace

The first attempt by the English to colonize "Virginia" was on Roanoke Island in the 1580's in this watercolor map by John White. (Engraved by Theodor de Bry in 1590 from Thomas Hariot's Admiranda Narratio fida tamen, de Commodis et Incolarum Ritibus Virginiae, *Frankfurt [1590])*

with Spain that followed Elizabeth's ascent, Sir John Hawkins embarked on the first of three slave-taking expeditions to the Spanish possessions in the Caribbean area.

Then came the globe-circling exploits of Sir Francis Drake and the north-west-passage explorations, at the same time, by Sir Martin Frobisher in Labrador. English businessmen backed such efforts in hopes of trade with newly opened regions. Various business enterprises were established: the Levant Company in 1582, the Venice Company in 1583, and the East India Company in 1600.

In each case, individuals and companies, yielding the capital to buy or rent ships, bought shares in the enterprise. All these ventures were private enterprises, created primarily for profit rather than for national growth or the placing of colonies.

But there were some Englishmen who saw the advantage of government-sponsored colonization, and chief among them were Sir Humphrey Gilbert and his half brother, Sir Walter Raleigh. In his *Discourse to prove a Passage by the North West to Cathaia*, which he presented to the Queen in 1574, Gilbert and his

Sir Walter Raleigh urged that England settle colonists overseas to strengthen and enrich the nation. (From the National Park Service, Colonial National Historical Park)

silent collaborator, Raleigh, argued the value of permanent overseas settlements and asked permission to plant them. The Queen agreed, and Sir Humphrey made two voyages on behalf of his project before being lost at sea on a homeward trip from Newfoundland in 1583. As his tiny ten-ton ship, the *Squirrel*, went down in a raging storm, Sir Humphrey was heard by the crew abroad the consort vessel gallantly consoling his men, "We are as near to heaven by sea as by land."

Sir Walter Raleigh took up where Sir Humphrey had left off in encouraging overseas English colonization. Raleigh once had been a favorite of Queen Elizabeth—some said a lover—until he had compromised her lady-in-waiting, Elizabeth

Sir Humphrey Gilbert, half-brother of Sir Walter Raleigh, was the first Englishman to attempt to settle a colony in North America and was lost at sea in 1583. (From the National Maritime Museum, Greenwich, England)

Throckmorton, and married her. He was still a man of influence and following in the lusty world of Elizabethan London. As poet he was often in the company of Shakespeare and that galaxy of Elizabethan writers whose fame shines through the ages. As courtier, he knew the powerful men of Court, Parliament, and the City of London. All his life he had hoped to colonize the New World and, as he put it, to plant "a new English nation in Virginia."

In 1584 Raleigh received from the Queen a hard-sought patent similar to Gilbert's. It empowered him "to discover and to plant Christian inhabitants in places convenient upon those large and ample countries extended northward from the cape of Florida, not in the actual possession of any Christian prince." The patent defined the claim as the unexplored lands between latitudes 34 and 45 degrees North, which extends from the present Cape Fear, in North Carolina, to the upper boundary of Maine.

To England's claim, Raleigh gave the name Virginea or Virginia, in honor of Her Virgin Majesty. The choice of the name was an inspired one, for England's admiration for her Queen extended almost to worship. Paintings and statues depicted her with the garb and beatific mien of the Virgin Mary, and poets apostrophized her as England's savior.

The three voyages that Raleigh undertook, beginning in 1584, were the first systematic attempt by the English to study and to colonize North America. This first was to explore the land lying behind the Outer Banks of the present North Carolina, a chain of islands stretching from Cape Lookout northward almost to the Virginia Capes, and find a suitable site to plant a settlement. The second effort under the command of Ralph Lane, in 1585–86, was the try by 108 men to colonize the area they called "the Cittie of Raleigh." Among the men in the group was gentleman artist John White, whose drawings provide the only surviving element of the colony. After a fight with the Indians, Lane decided to abandon the effort and left just days before Sir Richard Grenville arrived at Roanoke Island with supplies. Grenville left 15 men at the "Cittie," which was really no more than a crude fort, and returned to England.

The third desperate venture, in 1587, was intended to renew the colony and build a permanent settlement. One hundred and fifty men, women and children left Plymouth on May 8, 1587, for "Virginia." After a stormy voyage, the colonists arrived at Roanoke Island on July 23 and found the fort deserted. On this trip, John White was the leader (governor) of the settlement. About four weeks after the arrival, his daughter Eleanor, wife of Ananias Dare, a colleague of White, gave birth to Virginia Dare, the first child born of English parents in the New World.

White sailed on August 23, 1587, for England to get supplies, telling the colonists he would return before Christmas, but because of the war with Spain and the later attack by the Spanish Armada in the spring of 1588, there was an unplanned interlude in the re-supply of the colony. Raleigh finally was able to mount a relief expedition led again by White that arrived on Roanoke on August 15, 1590. To the bewilderment of the rescuers and of posterity,

Queen Elizabeth I wanted to challenge the Spanish and their colonies in America and supported the efforts of Sir Walter Raleigh. (From the editor's collection)

hardly a trace of the settlers could be found except for "CRO" carved on a tree and a single word, "Croatoan," on a post at the fort.

The Roanoke settlers found no re-supply ships coming to their aid because of the attack of the Spanish Armada. When supply ships finally returned in 1590, the fort was found deserted and the colonists gone. Carvings on a tree and a post in the stockade indicated the word "Croatoan" for a native tribe nearby. (From Pioneers in the Settlement of America *[1876])*

Where was White's family and where did the colonists go? Some have speculated they went south from Roanoke to join with the more friendly Croatoan Indians. Noted Williamsburg archaeologist, writer and historian Ivor Noël Hume in his 1994 book *The Virginia Adventure—Roanoke to James Towne, An Archaeological and Historical Odyssey* wrote: "Reports and rumors picked up by the seventeenth-century James Towne colonists strongly indicated that some [of the Roanoke Settlers] had gone north and that after their men folk had been killed by the Indians, women and children survivors were absorbed into tribes living south of the James River."

Whatever their destination, they were never seen again and forever became "The Lost Colony." ⚜

Virginia—The English Heritage in America, Hastings House Publishers, New York, 1966

CHAPTER 3 ❧

The English Challenge Spain's Claim

Elizabeth did not live to see England's standard permanently planted in the New World, but the event did not long follow her death. When the great Queen died at Richmond Palace in 1603 and King James VI of Scotland was called to London to become James I of England, other Virginia ventures were already under way. Raleigh sent out one last forlorn expedition in 1602 under Samuel Mace, who "performed nothing, but returned with idle stories and frivolous allegations." In the next two years, three other English expedi-

King James I of England encouraged the Virginia Company to send settlers to Virginia. (From the editor's collection)

tions explored parts of Virginia, one under Bartholomew Gosnold, one under Martin Pring, and a third under Bartholomew Gilbert, son of the ill-fated Sir Humphrey Gilbert. None contributed greatly to the sum of knowledge on Virginia.

A more colorful voyage, however, was made by George Weymouth in 1605 to North Virginia, as the New England area was called, bringing back five Indians to excite the interest of London's masses in the activities of the New World. A popular comedy, *Eastward Ho*, produced in London in 1605 with interpolations by Ben Johnson, also spread what was called "the Virginia fever."

Audiences gasped at Captain Seagull's description of Virginia to his two companions in a London tavern scene:

"I tell thee, gold is more plentiful there than copper is with us; and for as much red copper as I can bring, I'll have thrice the weight in gold. Why, man, all their dripping-pans... are pure gold; and all

their chains with which they chain up their streets are massy gold. All the prisoners
they take are fettered in gold; and for rubies and diamonds they go forth on holidays

*Sir Thomas Smythe, a leading London businessman,
headed the Virginia Company that dispatched 105
colonists to Virginia. (From the collection of the
Jamestown-Yorktown Foundation)*

and gather 'em by the seashore to
hang on their children's coats, and
stick in their children's caps, as commonly as our children wear saffron-gilt
breeches and groats with holes in 'em."

Four editions of this hit play
were published in four months. They
greatly stimulated interest in overseas
settlement, as well they might!

In 1606 King James I granted to
a group of London investors the charter under which England's first
permanent settlement was to be established. The Virginia Company of
London was headed by Sir Thomas
Smythe, the leading London businessman of his day, and its stock was
variously bought by wealthy nobles, by
merchants, and by London's powerful
city companies, which had evolved
from trade guilds in the Middle Ages
into fraternal bodies with philan-

thropic and promotional aims. For a subscription of 12 pounds and 10 shillings
—about $900 by today's standards—the company offered to make the investor "lord
of 200 acres of land," to be issued "to him and his heirs forever."

The company leased from the Muscovy Company two small merchant vessels
recently engaged in coal shipment from the British Isles to Russia, and it engaged
Christopher Newport, who had crossed the Atlantic nearly a dozen times, and
Bartholomew Gosnold, also a veteran sailor, as two of its captains. A call was sent out
for men to make the voyage and to remain in Virginia as colonists.

The charter of the company defined the limits of Virginia's coast in the same
terms as Queen Elizabeth's to Raleigh twenty-two years before, with the hope of
avoiding conflict with "other Christian princes." The Spanish remained in Florida, and
a French settlement had just been made, in 1605, to the north at Acadia, or Nova
Scotia. The western limit of Virginia was defined as 100 miles inland of the seacoast,
which was amended in a second charter in 1609 to read "from sea to sea."

Despite the findings of Hernando de Soto and Francisco Coronado, of Spain,
that a continuous land mass stretched from Florida to California, King James and his
advisers believed a tributary of the Chesapeake Bay could be found that would lead

through a narrow land mass to "the South Sea," or Pacific. Full realization of North America's vast extent did not reach England for a hundred years after Virginia had been settled.

The sector of Virginia assigned by King James for settlement by the Virginia Company of London extended from what is now lower North Carolina to Maine, with the most northern area later being assigned to the Virginia Company of Plymouth.

Preparations for the voyage did not escape notice of Spain, though the two nations technically had been at peace since 1604. In a coded message from London in 1606, Spain's ambassador warned his king, Philip III: "They propose to do another thing, which is to send five or six hundred men, private individuals of this kingdom, to people Virginia in the Indies, close to Florida." The ambassador also confronted Sir John Popham, Chief Justice of England, with this report and informed him that such a settlement would encroach on Spanish territory and violate the treaty. The Chief Justice explained that he favored the expedition only to rid England of thieves by drowning them.

However, prospect of a Virginia settlement so alarmed Philip that he asked his councilors how to deal with it. When the Spanish Board of War of the Indies advised that "with all necessary forces this plan of the English should be prevented," King Philip had his ambassador in London obtain an audience with King James and present objections. James I promised only to "look into the matter," and the offended ambassador advised Philip to drive the English out of Virginia, "hanging them in time which is short enough for the purpose."

King Philip III of Spain refused to take action against the Virginia colony. (From Wikipedia)

Philip's councilors also urged that he send a naval force against Virginia, but Philip refused to act. Perhaps memory of the Armada was still too strong. Whatever the cause, Spain missed her chance in 1606–1607 to destroy the seed of England in the New World at the moment of planting. She was to regret her indecision. ✤

Virginia—The English Heritage in America, Hastings House Publishers, New York, 1966

CHAPTER 4 ❧

The Ships of the Jamestown Era

When the Virginia voyagers embarked from Blackwall in 1606, they sailed aboard ships similar in design to Roman galleys of Nero's day. Through the Dark and Middle Ages, Europe had clung to the belief that a seagoing ship should be shaped like a whale, with a captain's castle looming high over its stern.

Like the personal metal armor the settlers brought with them to Jamestown, their cumbersome ships were a remnant of medievalism in the modern world.

These ships' design had evolved around the Mediterranean basin hundreds of years before Jamestown: the broad bow trailing off to a narrow stern, the high afterpeak to elevate captain above crew, the square-rigged sails of linen flax, the hull brightly decorated in the monarch's colors.

When English crusaders had visited the Holy Land in the twelfth century, they had taken home to England these ideas to superimpose on their own small fore-and-aft-rigged vessels. They learned more from subsequent contact with Venice, Genoa, and Spain. Spanish vessels taken as prizes by Sir Francis Drake from the Armada in 1588 were models for English ships to come.

The sea has strong traditions. The *Susan Constant*, *Godspeed*, and *Discovery*, ships that sailed to Virginia, were only small merchant vessels (though they may have sailed in the train of the British men-of-war that repelled the Armada), but

Seventeenth-century ships of the Jamestown era often were the great ships similar to this one. (From the Library of Radio Times-Hulton, London through the courtesy of the Old Dominion Foundation to the Jamestown-Yorktown Foundation)

each had its quarterdeck at the stern, like its medieval counterpart, from which its captain could dominate his ship.

Crew's quarters on the *Susan Constant* and *Godspeed* were on the main deck, forward and aft of the hatch, while passengers survived as best they could in the five-foot deep hold below the main deck; on the *Discovery* all crewmen bunked below-deck with the passengers. The five-foot ceiling caused many bumped heads.

In 1607 and for years after, the power of the captain was almost unlimited. The very location of his quarterdeck proclaimed him undisputed monarch. On board the narrow *Susan Constant*, Captain Christopher Newport had the luxury of two cabins, although all passengers lived in the hold together. If Newport were compassionate or greedy, he could give or rent space in one of his cabins to favored or wealthy passengers. Then, as today, the captain kept close to his charts and navigational instruments, including quadrant, astrolabe, cross staff, back staff, compass nocturnal, and a sand glass for measuring the time on each course and thus reckoning his position.

The *Susan Constant*, *Godspeed*, and *Discovery* had hauled coal between

Shipbuilding and shipping were vital to the English economy and defense of the nation in the seventeenth century. (From Pieter Van der Aa's Voyagien *(top) and Wenceslaus Hollar's* Navium Varie Figurae Et Formae *[1647])*

Muscovy and England before they were chartered by the Virginia Company. They were wider and slower than fighting ships, their length being only twice their beam, whereas the scale for men-of-war was three to one.

As protection against sea raiders and pirates, the *Susan Constant* and the *Godspeed* carried small guns, but they were no match for men-of-war. They also were much smaller than fighting ships, for some English men-of-war that fought the Armada were as large as 1,100 tons, while Spanish ships were even larger. Smallest of all was the *Discovery*, a pinnace, or sloop, usually engaged in coastal shipping.

The three ships bearing Virginia's first settlers sailed from Blackwall docks on the Thames River at London in December 1606. Sir Walter Raleigh who initiated the Roanoke voyages 20 years earlier was imprisoned in the Tower of London (far right) at that time. (A Sidney E. King drawing from A Pictorial Story of Jamestown, Virginia - The voyage & search for a settlement site, *copyrighted by J. Paul Hudson, 1957)*

The *Discovery's* helmsman controlled his ship by a single tiller, but the *Susan Constant* and *Godspeed* had to be steered by a whipstaff. Their helmsmen stood on a flat in a vertical box shaped like a coffin, part of which projected above the quarter-deck. Looking out through this hutch, a few inches above deck level, he controlled the rudder by moving the vertical whipstaff sidewise in front of him. This pole was pivoted on the deck below and was capable of moving the rudder with relatively little pressure from the helm. Thus, the helmsman also kept dry during rain and heavy seas.

Because of their draft and immense weight, the Jamestown ships were much more difficult to steer than the finer-line clipper ships that followed two centuries later. To compare them is to compare the whale with the shark. The virtue and strength of the merchantman lay in its broad beam and heavy timbers, which robbed it of speed but resisted overturning or foundering. From its reconstruction, it can be observed that even a relatively small seventeenth-century ship like the *Susan Constant* drew 12 feet of water.

When ships of Newport's day were under way or weather was rough, crew and passengers usually made their meal of hardtack and corned meat or of gruel composed of meal, water, and alcoholic spirits. However, fair weather permitted rations to be cooked on deck over a galley of brick and mortar. Sailors and crew often contracted scurvy or dysentery from unbalanced diet or spoiled food. The miasmic stench that arose from unpumped bilges caused other ill effects. No sanitary facilities were provided except the open latticework "head" at the forepeak of the vessel. If worse came to worst, the victim got a sea burial.

It is difficult to overestimate the importance of Drake's defeat of the Armada in giving England the ships and confidence with which to settle North America. In its wake Queen Elizabeth was proclaimed "Restorer of the Naval Power and Sovereign of the North Seas," recognizing her vigorous espousal of the Royal Navy and merchant marine. No less had been contributed by her grandfather, Henry VII, who had given England its first adequate national navy, and her father, the colorful Henry VIII, who had made the navy a force independent of the army.

In Elizabeth's long reign, English ships had finally broken the monopoly of Venice, Genoa, and Spain in the Mediterranean. In the same period of growth, Gerardus Mercator's chart of the world was completed, the art of navigation was developed, English rivers and harbors were charted, and the science of hydrography was born. All these helped bridge the seas to Jamestown. 🜍

The Iron Worker, Winter 1963–1964, Lynchburg Foundry Company

Ship Running out of Harbour *is the title of this late sixteenth-century Pieter Breughel rendering. (From the Library of Radio Times-Hulton, London through the courtesy of the Old Dominion Foundation to the Jamestown-Yorktown Foundation)*

The three ships—The Susan Constant, Godspeed, *and* Discovery—*maneuvering for anchorage off Jamestown Island in 1607 (From Griffith Bailey Coale painting in the Virginia Capitol, courtesy of the Library of Virginia)*

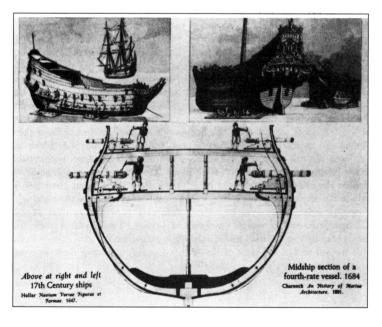

The merchant ships that brought the settlers to Jamestown were similar to the heavy-timbered vessels show in these seventeenth-century engravings. (From the Rouse Collection, Special Collections, Earl Gregg Swem Library, College of William and Mary)

CHAPTER 5

The English Voyage to Jamestown

Even by the standards of their time the *Susan Constant, Godspeed,* and *Discovery* were not large ships. To bring the three of them together across the Atlantic Ocean in winter was a difficult feat in 1607, as it would be today.

Yet English seamanship had been famous since the days of the Vikings, and English shipbuilders had learned during the recent Elizabethan age to combine the speed of their slender North Sea vessels with the magnificent size of galleons they had seen in Mediterranean waters in England's widening commerce during the reign of the great Queen Elizabeth. By their crushing defeat of the Spanish Armada, English sailors had conclusively shown themselves to be the masters of any sea-going men in Europe.

Now in 1606 they were sailing to follow up their Spanish victory with a claim to North American lands, in defiance of the decree of Pope Alexander VI, who in 1493 had divided the New World between the Roman Catholic monarchs of Spain and Portugal.

It was far from their first attempt. Sir Walter Raleigh had tried some years before and the English flag had reached North America again when English fishermen spent several summers along the Maine coast, but no permanent settlement had come out of it.

The Virginia Company chose winter for its voyage in order to put the settlers ashore in Virginia at planting time. From the several dozen previous English voyages to North America, they knew the outward passage would take from four to five months, using the preferred South Atlantic crossing. (The return would be quicker because of favorable Gulf Stream winds.)

Into the lower hold of the *Susan Constant,* the 100-ton flagship of the force, the crew stowed oats, barley, and wheat (they called it "corn") for seed. Building tools and farm implements were part of the cargo, together with beer and wine and the makings of the watery gruel that was to feed crew and passengers on the long voyage out.

Also aboard were cumbersome matchlock muskets, gunpowder, metal breast-plates, and helmets for protection. There were altar vessels, bibles, and prayer books for spiritual comfort, and beads and baubles for barter with the Indians; and build-

The Colonists leaving England for Jamestown, December 1606. (From a postal card by Jamestown Amusement & Vending Co., Inc. of Norfolk for the 1907 Jamestown Exposition, courtesy of the editor)

ing tools and farm implements for survival. The heavy helmets and breastplates were relics of medieval combat, no longer needed in Europe since the advent of gunpowder and the ponderous matchlock gun. However, earlier explorers had found them effective against Indian arrows.

It was one of the ironies of history that Raleigh, a prisoner in the Tower of London because of a suspected conspiracy against King James, could not see the history-making ships as they sailed on the outbound tide down the Thames for the English Channel and the open sea. A bend in the Thames between Blackwall, whence the ships sailed, hid them from his view, but no doubt he heard the news from his jailers. Perhaps Captain Christopher Newport, in command of the force, had consulted him on the best route to avoid the dread South Atlantic "horse latitudes" (so called later because of the loss of livestock in its becalmed waters), or how to deal with red Indians. To Raleigh, who first dreamed of "a new English nation" in North American, this voyage was to be a vindication.

Records of the passage are sketchy. The fullest account was written by George Percy, a younger son of the Duke of Northumberland, who remained at Jamestown until 1612. On December 20, 1606, "the fleet fell from London," Percy wrote. After a slow voyage down the Thames, past Queen Elizabeth's erstwhile palace at Greenwich, they finally reached the English Channel and anchored on January 5, 1607, in the Downs.

Says Percy: "The winds continued contrarie so long that we were forced to stay there some time, where we suffered great stormes, but by the skilfulnesse of the

Captaine we suffered no great losse or danger." In these agonizing weeks, when diminishing supplies threatened to end the voyage, Chaplain Robert Hunt inspired his shipmates by refusing to turn back in spite of deathly seasickness.

After six weeks, the weather improved and Captain Christopher Newport in the *Susan Constant* gave signal to Captain Bartholomew Gosnold in the *Godspeed* and John Ratcliffe in the *Discovery* to set sail southward, along the coasts of France and Spain. It was a monotonous voyage. On February 12, the crewmen on watch (passengers stayed below for fear of rheumy night air) saw a falling ("blazing") star, followed by a storm. A day or so later the ships put in at the Canary Islands to fill their water casks.

Then, just below the Tropic of Cancer, Newport changed course and the ships veered from the African coast and headed westward across the Atlantic: On March 23, more than three months out of London, "we fell with the Illand Mattanenio" (Martinique) in the West Indies. The first half of the voyage was safely past.

How could three sailing ships of different size and speed have kept together on so long an ocean voyage? The question remains unresolved to this day. No accounts left by the crew or passengers reveal the technique. Perhaps the 100-ton *Susan Constant* towed the 20-ton *Discovery* and thus enabled the 40-ton *Godspeed* to keep pace. It is known, however, that in the sixteenth-century English navy, an admiral's ship carried a cresset astern in which lightwood was burned at night to guide accompanying vessels. Perhaps Newport used some such device with his merchant ships, though it could only have been of slight help. Whatever the case, the crews showed

The Customs House (left) on the Thames River at London was near the departure point of many English sailing adventures, like the Jamestown voyage of 1606-1607. (From an engraving by Thomas Bowles for publisher Carrington Bowles in St. Paul's Church Yard)

superb seamanship in crossing relatively uncharted waters together and with no loss of life.

In rapid sequence, Newport's force put in at Dominicia, Guadeloupe, Nevis, Mona, and Montio. It was a welcome change indeed for the 105 passengers, who had spent three months sleeping in dark holds, to walk on solid earth. At Dominicia on March 24, natives brought them pineapples, potatoes, bananas, tobacco, and leather in return for knives, hatchets, beads, and copper jewelry. Two days later they sighted the small island of Marie Galante, and on March 27 they visited Guadeloupe Island and were fascinated by a hot spring that cooked pork in a half-hour.

On March 27 to 28 Newport sailed his ships past the then uninhabited islands of Montserrat and St. Kitts and landed at Nevis, where passengers and part of the crew camped six days. Then back to sea on April 4, past the islands of St. Eustatius and Sava, and another that Percy called the "Ile of Virgines," probably St. John or St. Thomas.

George Percy, son of the Duke of North-umberland, was among the colonists on the Jamestown voyage and kept a diary of the trip and early life in the settlement. (From the Virginia Historical Society)

On past Vieques and Puerto Rico they sailed to tiny Mona, where occurred the death of Edward Brooke, the first of the settlers to lose his life in the enterprise. Percy recorded that after a journey over the island's rocky terrain, Brooke's "fat melted within him by the greate heate and drought of the Country." On April 9, a small party of the settlers went by rowboat from Mona to the nearby island of Monito and brought back to their ship two hogsheads full of wildfowl and eggs.

Thus provisioned and refreshed, the settlers turn north and began the final crucial leg of their journey. A spring squall hit them on April 21, and the ships lowered sail to avert grounding, believing them near the coast of Virginia. Their hopes were premature, however, for five days must pass before they would see its headlands. "The six and twentieth day of Aprill," wrote Percy, "about foure a 'clocke in the morning, wee descried the Land of Virginia; the same day wee entred into the Bay of Chesupioc [Chesapeake] directly..." The day was Sunday, April 26, 1607.

As the sun rose over dark waters, sailors could make out the low, pine-forested shore of Virginia, which poet Michael Drayton had ambitiously proclaimed "earth's only paradise." Landing on a promontory, they cautiously explored the rim of the

After first arriving in Virginia waters, the settlers went ashore on April 26, 1607 and encountered hostile natives. (A Sidney E. King sketch from **A Pictorial Story of Jamestown, Virginia - The voyage & search for a settlement site,** *copyrighted by J. Paul Hudson, 1957)*

Chesapeake Bay. Percy was entranced with "faire medowes and goodly tall trees, with such Fresh-waters turning through the woods, as I was almost ravished at the fight sight thereof." But pleasure turned to pain when Indians suddenly emerged and drove the exploring party back aboard ship, wounding settler Gabriel Archer and sailor Mathew Morton. Such was the settlers' ominous welcome to Virginia.

During the 10 weeks under sail (February to April), Newport had been the unquestioned master of the ships, the 39 seamen and the settlers, now reduced to 104 by Brooke's death. However, that evening at Cape Henry the sealed box of instructions from the Virginia Company was opened, and Newport was forced to share his primacy with Gosnold and Ratcliffe, together with Edward Maria Wingfield, John Martin, George Kendall, Captain John Smith, the most controversial hero in all American legend, and several others. No longer could Newport reign supreme; hereafter he must abide by the wishes of the quarrelsome Council.

Thus, in Virginia's April of redbud and dogwood, the Argonauts reached their goal. So rich and numerous were Virginia's charms that they were filled with desire to hasten ashore and find the gold and jewels which must abound in so favored a country.

Exploring parties busily reconnoitered the area: Virginia Beach on April 27, and Lynnhaven Inlet and Point Comfort on April 28. On Wednesday, April 29, they erected a cross and gave thanks to God on the land where they stood, naming it Cape Henry in honor of one of the sons of King James.

On April 30 they hoisted sail and headed up the James, following it instead of

A view of Jamestown Island from a nearby marsh was taken recently, but it could well be a view nearly 400 years ago because the island is still marshy and heavily vegetated. (From the Newport News **Daily Press,** *photo by Scott DeMuesy)*

the Chesapeake Bay, in anticipation of finding the long hoped-for westward passage through North America to the Pacific. They also were obeying instructions from His Majesty's Council for Virginia to settle 30 or 40 miles upriver from the Atlantic so that coast-watchers, later stationed at Point Comfort, could warn the colony by runner if Spanish marauders approached.

To explore the shoals of the James, too shallow for the ships, the settlers used a shallop or rowboat, brought from England in sections and assembled at Cape Henry. At each protected place until they reached the confluence of the Appomattox, at what is now Hopewell, the ships paused while the shallop nosed ashore, seeking a deep-water landing. Then, dissatisfied, they went back downriver and examined a point near the present Williamsburg, which Gabriel Archer so championed they named it "Archer's Hope." They rejected it because supply ships "could not ride neere the shoare," but next day found a peninsula two miles away with water so deep their vessels could approach its banks.

Mooring the weary ships to trees overhanging the river, the settlers prepared to go ashore. The long voyage was over. On May 13, 1607, the site for Jamestown was found.

Next day the 104 settlers left the ships and began to build the triangular palisade that was to be England's first permanent settlement overseas. While the Council elected Wingfield president, others cleared a site and cut clapboard as cargo for the ship's return voyage. In a few days English wheat, oats, and barley were germinating beneath the alien earth in small clearings around the camp.

A feeling of optimism surged through the settlement. Captain Newport felt that

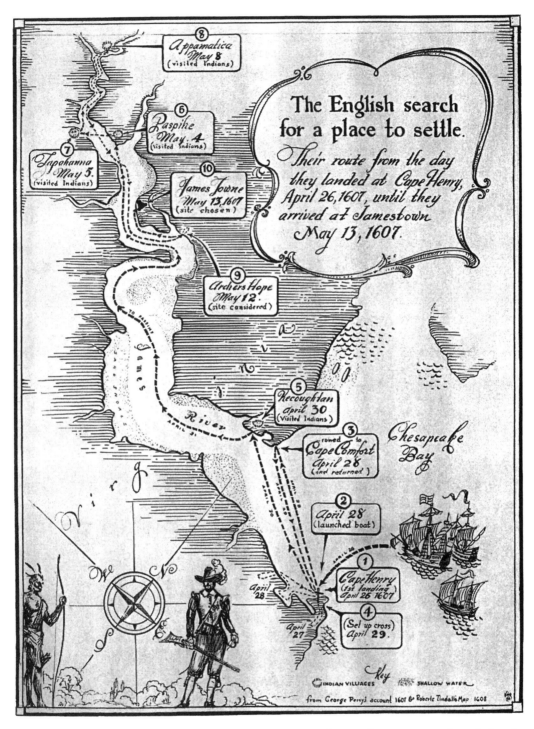

The Jamestown ships landed in Virginia on April 26, 1607 and spent the next two weeks exploring the James River area before landing at Jamestown Island on May 13, 1607. (A Sidney E. King drawing from A Pictorial Story of Jamestown, Virginia - The voyage & search for a settlement site, *copyrighted by J. Paul Hudson, 1957)*

On April 29, 1607 the settlers landed at a point of land they called Cape Henry and set up a cross, according to George Percy's diary account. (A Sidney E. King drawing in **A Pictorial Story of Jamestown, Virginia - The voyage & search for a settlement site,** *copyrighted by J. Paul Hudson, 1957, from the painting by Stephen Reid, Chrysler Museum of Art)*

the "new English nation overseas" also had begun to germinate, and on June 22, he ordered his crews back to two of the ships and set sail for England, leaving the *Discovery* for the colonists' use in their vain search for the elusive westward passage.

Although the *Susan Constant* and *Godspeed* were to return to the New World as supply ships, they were never again to make so historic a voyage as that to Virginia in 1606–07. As the British political scientist Sir James Bryce declared three centuries later, "The landing at Jamestown was one of the great events in the history of the world—an event to be compared for its momentous consequences with the overthrow of the Persian empire by Alexander; with the destruction of Carthage by Rome; with the conquest of Gaul by Clovis; with the taking of Constantinople by the Turks—one might almost say with the discovery of America by Columbus..." ⚜

The Iron Worker, Winter 1963–1964, Lynchburg Foundry Company

CHAPTER 6

The Indians
Before Jamestown

When the English settlers first touched Virginia on April 26, 1607, an exploring party went ashore at Cape Henry and was entranced by what they saw. But danger for them lurked in the midst of beauty. Out of the pinewoods that rimmed Chesapeake Bay darted naked Indian warriors.

Before the Englishmen could flee in their shallop, the tribesmen had wounded two men—Gabriel Archer and Mathew Morton.

This was the first meeting with the Indians who had lived along Virginia's shores since the shadowy centuries before the fateful voyages of Columbus. It was a symbolic meeting. Many Englishmen would die before Virginia was fully settled. And, in spite of the settlers' lurking sense of guilt, they would kill or displace most of Virginia's tribes before the land was theirs.

The English expected to find Indians as mild as the indolent Caribs of the West Indies. They knew that Spanish conquistadors had killed and enslaved the South American tribes, but they ascribed this to cruelty. Their instructions from the Virginia Company were to befriend the Indian and obtain help in finding gold and the westward passage to the South Sea. They expected even to create Indian schools and to convert the natives to Christianity, as faithful subjects of the King. They suffered from the romantic delusion that man in his native state was a "noble savage." Yet the settlers ended by exploiting the Indians, just as they themselves

Indian Warriors, like this one, hunted and fished the lower James River area around Jamestown. (Engraved by Theodor de Bry in 1590 from Thomas Hariot's **Admiranda Narratio fida tamen, de Commodis et Incolarum Ritibus Virginiae,** Frankfurt, [1590])

Algonquin warriors, depicted by artist John White, were much like those seen by the Jamestown settlers. (Engraved by Theodor de Bry in 1590 from Thomas Hariot's Admiranda Narratio fida tamen, de Commodis et Incolarum Ritibus Virginiae, *Frankfurt, [1590])*

were exploited later by British colonial policy.

The Europeans on their arrival in Virginia were fascinated with Indian culture, and men such as John Smith and William Strachey were inspired to write full accounts of Indian life for publication in England. George Percy, Henry Spelman (a hostage to the Indians for one Jamestown winter), and Gabriel Archer left other helpful information. In 1705 Robert Beverley's *History and Present State of Virginia* devoted its third section to an account of Indian customs and the tragic effect of European civilization on Indian life.

When the Jamestown settlers arrived, the present area of Virginia was inhabited by a large number of tribes from three linguistic stocks: Algonquian, Iroquoian, and Siouan. Of these, the Algonquians were in most constant contact with the settlers because they occupied the coastal and Tidewater areas, east of a line running south from the District of Columbia through Fredericksburg, Richmond, Petersburg, and then along the Blackwater River and into North Carolina as far south as the Neuse River. They also held the territory on the Eastern Shore in what is now Accomack and Northampton counties.

Anthropologists surmise that the Algonquians pushed down into Virginia from the North hundreds of years before the English came. By 1607 they had been organized into a confederacy of more than two dozen tribes with Wahunsonacock—known to the colonists as Powhatan—as the principal or great chief. Six of these tribes—the Powhatan, Arrohattoc, Appomattox, Mattaponi, Pamunkey, and Youngtanund—he had inherited. The others he won over by force or threat.

Smith lists in his *Travels & Works* 32 tribes of the Powhatan "empire," but he shows 36 "king's houses" on his first map of Virginia. Throughout these provinces Smith located 161 Indian villages. Over these people, estimated to number about 9,000, Powhatan held the power of life and death.

Beneath Powhatan, heading each of the sub-tribes, was a local chief or werowance. Each tribe gave allegiance and paid tribute to Powhatan, and there were farmlands and shallow water fishing areas that were proper to each Indian town. Such tribute, in the form of corn and beans, deerskins and copper, and beads and pearls, was collected annually like taxes and sent to Powhatan by its chief. Each chief, says Strachey, paid to Powhatan "eight parts of ten tribute of all the commodities which their country yieldeth."

Nobody knows for certain where these Indians came from. Archaeologists continue to dig up evidence that humans roamed the North American continent at least 16,000 years or more before the age of English, Spanish, and French exploration of North America. In fact, the recently-dug Cactus Hill site in Sussex County pushes human occupation of Virginia back to about 16,000 years ago—at least.

In recent years, archaeologists and anthropologists also have taken issue with the long-held premise that the first North Americans were descendants of ancient Asiatic people who crossed the Bering Strait land bridge from Asia to Alaska about 14,000 years ago. These Ice age primitives then made their migration into what is now the Old Dominion.

A growing school of scholars believes that, judging from stone spear points found across the United States, prehistoric Europeans may have migrated to North America even before Mongols came from Asia. These early tribesmen may have sailed across the ocean in some kind of craft.

These prehistoric weapons—some found in Tidewater Virginia—look more

An Indian man and woman eating from a large circular dish containing grains of food. In the fore-ground are other items, including a fish and ears of corn. (Engraved by Theodor de Bry in 1590 from Thomas Hariot's Admiranda Narratio fida tamen, de Commodis et Incolarum Ritibus Virginiae, *Frankfurt, [1590])*

like ancient European spear points than like those of the Mongols, archaeologists have surmised. The weapons, called "Clovis points," are so named because they were first found in ancient sites at Clovis, New Mexico. Radiocarbon tests on bones associated with the stone points identify them as being 12,000 years old and some of the oldest man-made objects identified in North America. In recent years much older, but less elegantly made, tools have been found in several regions, including Virginia.

Clovis points were first found in Virginia near Clarksville, on the Roanoke River, in the 1940s. There, National Park Service diggers excavated 78 Clovis points when they explored the remains of the one-time Indian trading island of the Occonneechee Indians. That was before the U.S. Government built Buggs Island Dam (officially the John H. Kerr Dam) on the Roanoke River and submerged that romantic island of prehistory under eight feet of water.

Clovis points were fluted or striated by the prehistoric tribesmen who made them. They were then bound to sticks and used as spears or projected as arrows. In fact, Clovis points look very much like the Indian arrowheads that many youngsters of my generation picked up on the James River shore in the 1920s and 1930s. Ordinary arrowheads lack the fluting or striation, however.

Since those first Clovis points were dated by high-tech methods in New Mexico in 1926, others have been found in Virginia and several eastern sites. Searches by the late Dr. Ben McCary, then a professor at the College of William and Mary and longtime archaeologist, and others, turned up 67 pre-Indian points years ago in Dinwiddie County.

So far no skull or skeleton of the Clovis man has been found, but research indicates that he knew how to use fire, throw a spear, and perhaps use a spear-thrower, or atlatl. He worked skillfully in stone but made no pottery. He knew nothing about growing food, but depended on wild plants and animals during his nomadic life. He was never numerous, but was forever on the move.

In successive millennia, descendants of Clovis man (also known as Paleo-Indian) refined his methods of hunting. The next clearly defined period in Virginia's prehistory is the Archaic, dating from 6,000 years to 800 years before Christ. Projectile points with straight stems or tapering bases replaced the fluted points of the Clovis type; hence a stone object known as the banner-stone or atlatl weight, attached to a throwing stick made its appearance. Apparently, Archaic man was learning how to catch fish more easily, though game and wild vegetables remained his chief source of food. He also developed the predecessor of pottery by making flat-bottomed vessels of soapstone. Pieces of this have been found in all parts of Virginia, from the Dismal Swamp to the Southwest, despite the fact that soapstone out-croppings are found in Virginia only in the Piedmont.

While the Paleo-Indian usually chose to camp along a large stream, the Archaic Indian usually chose a fill or slope. Campsites of this period are small but relatively numerous in Virginia. To the archaeologist's delight, they yield a large number of artifacts.

In the evolution of prehistoric North American man, the span of years from 800 B.C. to 1600 A.D., known as the Woodland Period, was a time of great change in human life. Nomadic prehistoric man apparently increased in number and confined his wanderings to a smaller orbit, leading to differentiation into the various tribes which English and Spanish explorers later found along the Atlantic coast in their sixteenth century explorations.

Because these people left no written record and today's oral history is mainly concerned with what has happened to their people since 1607, we must depend significantly on archaeology to reveal what transpired in Virginia before the English arrived. The Powhatans of 1607, however, said a number of things about their immediate past and author William Strachey wrote them down.

(*Editor's note*: For a long time, there were few skeletal remains found to help tell the story, but in the early 1990's across Virginia, a number were uncovered and analyzed and reports published. These skeletons also have been re-buried at the request of present-day Indian tribes.)

Unlike our own fast-changing times, man's technological progress was snail-like in these years, and many implements of the Archaic Period continued in use through the Woodland times. Wood, stone, and clay were his standby, for he was still unfamiliar with metal.

Indians along the James River used log canoes to pursue fish and for transportation. (Engraved by Theodor de Bry in 1590 from Thomas Hariot's Admiranda Narratio fida tamen, de Commodis et Incolarum Ritibus Virginiae, *Frankfurt, [1590])*

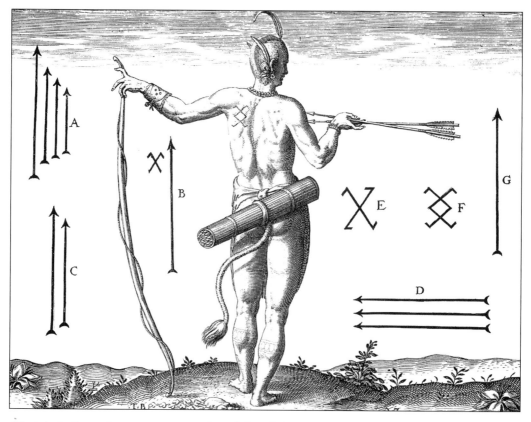

Virginia Indians often wore tattoos to show their tribal allegiance or place of origin. The seven designs pictured here were those seen by John White on his voyage to Roanoke. (Engraved by Theodor de Bry in 1590 from Thomas Hariot's Admiranda Narratio fida tamen, de Commodis et Incolarum Ritibus Virginiae, *Frankfurt, [1590])*

Early in this period, Virginia Indians began to made crude pottery of clay tempered with soapstone and later with sand or shell, consisting of pots and flat, rounded, or conoidal bottoms, with cord or net-malleated surfaces. Weapons and implements increased in number and variety in this period: large and roughly-ground celts (prehistoric tool) for hollowing log canoes, scrapers for preparing arrow shafts, pestles for grinding corn and seeds, drills for boring holes, hammer stones for hammering and crushing, and sinkers for lowering fish nets to the desired water depth. Some experts also believe that a grooved stone ax and three-quarter grooved ax extended into this period from the late Archaic.

The greatest cultural advance probably made during Archaic times was the introduction of the bow for use in projecting arrows—that utilized stemmed projectile points. Certainly, the next most important was the beginning of the cultivation of crops, especially by the Tidewater (the area eastward from the fall line of the rivers) Indians. Trade with Indians of other sections evidently began, for beads and shells from Indian sites elsewhere on the Atlantic Coast and along the Guilf of Mexico were found in Virginia.

In the last 500 or 600 years before the English came to Virginia, Indian populations greatly increased, and villages became larger and more permanent. The growing of corn and beans gave great certainty to life. The cultivation of Indian tobacco began, probably even before the introduction of corn and beans, and Tidewater Indians fashioned delicately made clay pipes that were probably the model for the first simple pipes developed by the English well after 1607. One type is easily recognized by decorations cut into the pipe bowl showing a deer or a chevron or star design. This pipe represents the finest product from the hands of any Eastern clay pipe maker. Indian smokers in the Piedmont region seem to have preferred pipes of soapstone.

"Peuples de Virginie" were portrayed in a seventeenth-century French engraving. (From Alain Manesson Mallet, Description de l'Univers, *Paris [1683])*

Campsites of late Woodland Period Indians in Virginia have yielded a rich reward of bone awls, needles, fishhooks, beads, flakes, and beamers for scraping hides. Seashells provided marginella beads, such as those that decorate the famous cloak of Chief Powhatan in the collection of the Ashmolean Museum at Oxford University (See chapter 30). From stone, the Indian continued to make mortars and pestles, spear and arrow points, and celts, or stone axes. Fragments of round-bodied pots with straight sides, or globular pots with rounded bases are common.

The white man on his arrival in Virginia was fascinated with Indian culture, and men such as John Smith and William Strachey were inspired to write full accounts of Indian life for publication in England, much like John White did earlier with his watercolors of the Roanoke area Indians. 🪶

The Iron Worker, Summer 1965, Lynchburg Foundry Company

The late Dr. Ben C. McCary, professor at the College of William and Mary, contributed to the original article.

CHAPTER 7 ❧

Captain Christopher Newport

W ho was Christopher Newport? In truth, he was the captain of the first English voyage to Jamestown, but John Smith and Pocahontas elbowed the one-armed seafarer, for a long time, out of history books. But no more.

Research by a number of British scholars reveals him as one of the bravest of the captains in the globe-girdling era of Queen Elizabeth I, who ruled England from 1558 to 1603.

After delivering the first permanent English settlers safely to Virginia, the bearded Newport made four follow-up trips to Virginia with passengers and supplies. His annual arrival was so eagerly awaited at Jamestown, historians say, that the entrance to the James River was soon known as "Newport's News," or Newport News.

Historians divide Newport's life into three careers, each packed with enough excitement for a James Bond thriller. Newport's first life was spent in the crew of English privateers that preyed on cargoes hauled by Spanish and French merchantmen. His second was his five-year employment as admiral by the Virginia Company of London from 1606 through 1611.

His last adventures were in the service of the East India Company, which had opened trading posts in the Orient to compete with the Portuguese and Dutch. It was on his third East India voyage that Newport died, age 57, in the port of Bantam (west of the present day Jakarta, Indonesia.)

One historian relates that Newport's exploits sound like Sinbad the Sailor's. He escaped death a dozen times, was once put ashore as a mutineer, and captured treasure ships many times larger than his own vessel.

Born in the poor Limehouse section of London, Newport first went to sea as a cabin boy. On an early voyage to Brazil, he was banished from the ship with two other discontented sailors and was lost to English eyes for several years. He might never have returned had he not been captured by a ship of the Earl of Cumberland and carried back to London.

He soon went back to sea, this time as captain of a privateer that sailed with England's famous Sir Francis Drake to Cadiz, Spain, in 1587, and attacked ships assembled there for the Spanish Armada's attempted invasion of England. This feat, which Drake described as "singeing the beard of the King of Spain," destroyed and captured more than 30 Spanish ships. It hastened Spain's end as a great power.

This gave Newport a taste for bigger hauls. So, he sailed as a captain of a (legitimate) privateer for the West Indies, to fight the Spanish silver-carrying ships. In one bitter battle, Newport lost his right arm. Undeterred by this loss, Newport spent 13 years plundering Spanish ships in the Caribbean. His biggest haul was taken in 1592 when his ship captured the Spanish carrack *Madre de Dios*, loaded with spices, gems, silks, and other goods valued at a half million pounds. Newport had to divide it with the Queen, the ship-owners, and his crew (as was the privateer's requirement of the day).

When the Spanish ship first appeared on the horizon, Newport summoned his men on deck and told them: "Masters, now the time is come that either we must end our days or take the said carrack." Then, according to his narrative, he "wished all the company to stand to their charge like men, and if any displeasure were amongst any of them, to forget and forgive one another, which everyone seems willing unto." After toasting each other's health, they attacked the Spanish and defeated them.

Christopher Newport was captain of the fleet of three ships that sailed to Jamestown. (From a mural by Allan D. Jones, Jr., Newport News Public Library, West Avenue Branch)

Captain Christopher Newport's embarkation for London several weeks after arriving at Jamestown. (From the collection of the Jamestown-Yorktown Foundation)

When the Virginia Company of London sought a man to command their flagship, the *Susan Constant*, and lead the *Godspeed* and *Discovery* to Virginia, it found that Newport knew the American coast better than anyone else. He had what one historian called "an unrivalled experience of the Atlantic crossing by the Canaries, of West Indies waters, and watering places, and of the Florida Channel and the homeward passage by Newfoundland or by Bermuda and the Azores."

Or as one of his contemporaries said, he was "a mariner well practiced for the western parts of America."

As master for the Virginia Company, Newport was responsible for the safety of all ships and passengers who traveled with him. In his six years of employment, he made five voyages from London to Virginia and return, encountering serious trouble only in 1609, when his ship the *Sea Venture* was wrecked at Bermuda. But Newport and others directed the building of two new ships and safely completed the voyage.

While in Virginia, he explored the James and other rivers for the company, trying to find one that would connect with the Pacific Ocean. He never could find it, for it did not exist.

Once Virginia seemed successfully planted, Newport was ready for a new adventure. He found it with the East India Company, whose stockholders he had known in the Virginia Company. So good a trader did he prove with the Orientals that the East India Company gave him a bonus of 50 gold coins, each worth about $6 at that time, besides his salary.

All went well until the third voyage, when the wiry captain's luck ran out and he died and was buried in Bantam. Recognizing his service, the Virginia Company gave his widow 3,500 acres of land in Virginia. ❀

Newport News *Daily Press,* August 6, 1967

The voyage's captain, Christopher Newport, regulated all activities of crew and settlers until the settlement was established at Jamestown. (A Sidney E. King drawing from A Pictorial Story of Jamestown, Virginia - The voyage & search for a settlement site, *copyrighted by J. Paul Hudson, 1957)*

CHAPTER 8 ✤

Jamestown: Capital of an Empire

Jamestown was the beginning of the American era in world history, but the securing of the beachhead was no easy achievement for those first settlers. Thousands of Englishmen lost their lives to establish a foothold in the swamp. Its career was the commencement of the American success story—from crude beginnings to great power.

In reality there were several Jamestowns from the beginning until the late nineteenth-century when it began to revert to wilderness and then was rescued, but those are different stories.

The first saga, centering in the three-cornered fort that the colonists began when they streamed ashore on May 14, 1607, was the critical twelve years from landing until the end of military rule under Governor Samuel Argall in 1619. It is the primitive Jamestown that most excites the imagination.

The vision of city-bred Londoners felling giant pines to build a palisade against Spanish and Indians warriors quickens the pulse of armchair adventurers. For ten years the colony's life hung by a thread. Once in 1610, settlers actually abandoned the accursed spot and sailed for home, only to get word before they reached the mouth of the James River at Hampton Roads that Lord Thomas West, Baron De la Warr, the colony's first governor, was arriving with settlers and supplies.

(*Editor's note*: Lord De la Warr initially remained in Virginia only one year, returning to England in 1611 and remaining until 1618 when he began his return voyage. He died en route. His name was given to the state of Delaware, the Delaware River, and an Indian tribe.)

The colonists followed the written directions of His Majesty's Council for Virginia that suggested a site about 40 miles upriver from the Virginia Capes for security against Spanish marauders.

The fort they built was largely triangular surrounded by a moat. Its river side was 420 feet long and its other two sides about 300 feet. At each corner was a bulwark built like a "halfe moone," on which "foure or five pieces of Artillerie" could be mounted. The fort is believed to have enclosed about one acre, with small dwellings paralleling the walls. From the rear bulwark flew England's flag, the large red Cross of St. George on a field of white.

To reduce the labor of hauling cargo, the fort was placed close to the shore. A dock was later built from its shore and named Sir Thomas Dale's bridge. The main gate opened onto the shore, while others were later added for convenience. The heavy planks that formed this palisade were cut on the site and embedded upright into the sandy earth.

(*Editor's note*: Archaeologists have recently uncovered portions of the old fort that showed much of it had not been lost to the river as earlier historians had feared.)

To shelter them for the first few weeks, settlers dug shallow caves or built lean-tos of cloth and branches. As soon as the palisade was reared, they built small houses at regular intervals inside its walls. By direction of His Majesty's Council, these were placed about 15 feet from the palisade to allow for a uniform street. At the triangle's center, the company built a church flanked by a guardhouse and a storehouse.

Buildings were framed of rough oak and pine and then covered with a lattice of grapevine and saplings. On this wattle was plastered a daub of mud and ground oyster shell, which hardened to form a waterproof surface. The roofs were reeds lashed together like the thatching of rural English houses of that day.

In spite of its simplicity, James Fort was impressive. A constant watch was at

The arrival of settlers to Jamestown in 1607 was fancifully portrayed in this contemporary print. There was no such greeting for the Englishmen. (From the American Heritage Publishing Co., Inc.)

first kept in the area between church, guardhouse, and storehouse, designated the
Court of Guard. Here steel-helmeted halberdiers, or pike men, stood guard against
Spanish and Indians. At night the gates were closed, and watchmen on the bulwarks
scanned river and woods for intruders. Although the cries of owls, whippoorwills, and
wildcats echoed through the woods, those inside could feel almost secure.

True to their Anglican belief, the settlers made their church and meetinghouse
the center of this England in America. In the months before its completion, their
minister, the Rev. Robert Hunt preached from a pulpit nailed between two trees with
a kind of canvas awning over it. In this open-air church they celebrated the first
recorded Protestant "communion" in the New World. Soon afterward Chaplain Hunt
was able to offer daily prayers in the church.

In Virginia's archives is a lengthy prayer said at the Court of Guard at each
change of watch. Believed to have been written by the Rev. William Crashaw in
England, it realistically pictures the settlers' plight:

"…We know, O Lord, we have the Devil and all the gates of Hell against us,
but if Thou, O Lord, be on our side, we care not who be against us. And, seeing by
Thy motion and work in our hearts, we have left our warm nests at home and put
our lives into Thy hands, principally to honor Thy name and advance the Kingdom

*The first place of worship at Jamestown was an area in the forest covered with tattered sailcloth,
described by John Smith in his recollections, and the pulpit was a bar of wood nailed to two nearby
trees. (From* Jamestown Church at Historic Jamestown, Virginia*)*

of Thy Son, Lord, give us leave to commit our lives into Thy hands... "

Simple as James Fort was, it took months to complete. At a sawpit outside the fort, artisans first sawed three trunks into framing timbers. Others smoothed the sawn surfaces with adzes and broad-axes. Nails were scarce and expensive. Instead the builders used *trunnels* (tree-nails), which were wooden wedges driven into bored holes to join timbers together.

Within days of reaching Jamestown, the colonists began to build a fort. (From the Julien Binford painting, courtesy of the Jamestown-Yorktown Foundation)

In the primitive style of Elizabethan artisans, the settlers let their timbers determine the size of their buildings. Foundations were paced off by foot, and shapes were irregular. Chinks were caulked with mud, reeds, and excelsior.

For lack of glass, windows were simply openings that could be shuttered. Hearth fire, smoldering reeds, or candles provided lighting.

Low floor sills and rain-soaked thatch roofs kept the buildings damp. This gave relief from heat in summer, but bred colds and rheumatism in winter. To offset it, each house had a small wattle-and-daub chimney. Fires were built in the first years on hearths in the center of huts, but later buildings boasted fireplaces. In either case, sparks easily ignited reed roofs and sapling walls. The settlers wrote often of fires which ravaged the fort and the village that grew up outside around it.

Furnishings of the fort dwellings were simple and homemade except for sea chests and perhaps church furniture. The only item thought to have survived is a chest, identified as Captain John Smith's, given many years ago to the state-owned Jamestown Festival Park (now Jamestown Settlement) and placed on exhibit.

Life in the fort had a military tempo. John Smith during his governorship drilled watch-standers in an area outside the palisade that came to be known as "Smithfield." Severe military law governed, and the death penalty was common. The fact is that early Jamestown was a military camp. English civil law was not in effect until Governor Yeardley in 1619 brought instruction from the Virginia Company in London to call an assembly and adopt the reforms that Sir Edwin Sandys had incorporated in his admirable Great Charter of 1618.

Virginia was first governed by ten councilors chosen by the Virginia Company in 1606. This, however, was not revealed until Captain Christopher Newport,

By the end of the first year, the Settlement at Jamestown included the fort, a blockhouse [or watchtower] and a glasshouse for the first industry. (From A Tryal of Glasse—The Story of Glassmaking at Jamestown, courtesy of Eastern National)

commander of the *Susan Constant*, opened the sealed instructions when the ships reached Cape Henry in April 1607. Besides Newport, who was in full command until the settlers were landed, the councilors were: Edward Maria Wingfield, president; Bartholomew Gosnold and John Ratcliffe, who commanded the *Godspeed* and *Discovery*; George Percy, younger son of the Duke of Northumberland; John Smith, who had fought as an adventurer in several European wars; and John Martin, George Kendall, Gabriel Archer, and the Rev. Robert Hunt.

Newport made use of the first weeks after the landing to explore the James River west to the fall line, at the present Richmond. He was following instructions from His Majesty's Council to seek a water route, which mariners believed would link North America's East Coast to the South Sea, as they called the Pacific Ocean. For the next two centuries, Virginians were to search in vain for this hoped-for passage that would lead them to Cathay, or China.

Unsuccessful in this quest, Newport and his 38 mariners obeyed company instructions and sailed for England on June 22, 1607, in the *Susan Constant* and *Godspeed*. The pinnace *Discovery*, a shallow-draft coastal vessel, remained behind for exploring and for trade with the Indians.

The settlers' hardships were numerous. William Simmonds compiled an account in London during this period from reports he received from colonists. Describing Wingfield's lusterless leadership, Simmonds wrote:

"Our drink was water, our lodging, castles in the air. With this lodging and diet, our extreme toil in bearing and planting palisades strained and bruised us. Our continual labor in the extremity of the heat had so weakened us as were cause sufficient to have made us miserable in our native country, or any other place in the world. From May to September those that escaped dying lived upon sturgeon and sea crabs. Fifty in this time were buried.

"Then seeing the President's projects (who all this time had neither felt want nor sickness) to escape these miseries by flight in our pinnace, so moved our dead spirits that we deposed him and established Ratcliffe in his place...but now was all our provisions spent, the sturgeon gone, all helps abandoned, each hour expecting the fury of the savages, when God, the patron of all good endeavors, in that desperate extremity, so changed the hearts of the savages that they brought such plenty of their fruits and provisions that no man wanted...

"The new president, being little beloved, of weak judgment in dangers and less industry in peace, committed the managing of all things abroad to Captain Smith, who, by his own example, good words, and fair promises set some to mow, others to build houses, others to thatch them, himself always bearing the greatest task for his own share. In short time he provided most of them lodgings, neglecting any for himself...

"And now the winter approaching, the rivers became so covered with swans, geese, ducks, and cranes that we daily feasted with good bread, Virginia pease, pumpkins, and persimmons, fish, fowl, and divers sorts of wild beasts... so that none of our Tuftaffaty humorist desired to go to England..."

From this and other accounts, it is clear that Smith's leadership brought order out of chaos. Once Newport departed in the ships, the bearded little captain proved the ablest of the councilors. It is no exaggeration to say that Smith saved Jamestown.

The settlement soon outgrew James Fort. The 15 original cottages each housed an average of seven men of the 104 settlers, and the cottages were tiny. Although death took a steady toll, the fort was no doubt overflowing with settlers by the time Newport returned to Jamestown in January 1608, with 120 more optimists in the first supply taskforce. Crowding increased in October with the arrival of the second supply of 170 persons.

By the time the third supply landed in August 1609, many settlers were building outside the cramped fort. Probably among these were the first women at Jamestown: Mrs. Forrest and her maid, Ann Burras, who had come in the Second Supply. So long as Jamestown remained a military garrison, immigra-

Efforts began almost immediately to coexist with the neighboring Indian tribes and meetings were held frequently. (From a postal card published by the Jamestown Amusement & Vending Co., Norfolk, for the 1907 Jamestown Exposition, courtesy of the editor)

tion of women to Virginia was discouraged. From 1608 until a shipload of maids came in 1620 to become brides, women were few. The hazards were too great.

Progress the first three years was slight. John Smith's trade with the Indians from 1607 to 1610 averted starvation. Creation of a glass factory manned by eight German and Polish glassblowers in 1608 was another show of confidence. Arrival of the third group of supply ships brought total immigration to 794 although 300 of this total were dead by the end of 1609.

Quickly, the Starving Time wiped out the costly gains of three years—the winter of 1609–10. Jamestown's 500 settlers were reduced in no time to 59. Ravenous men consumed horses, dogs, cats, rats, and mice. Why they did not eat oysters or fish is a mystery. The James River at Jamestown is too brackish to attract many fish, but they abounded in the salty tidal waters twenty miles down the James, towards the Atlantic.

The Starving Time and John Smith's return to England the same winter brought Jamestown to its lowest ebb. A third blow was the wreck of the Sea Venture at Bermuda en route to Jamestown. When Lieutenant Governor Sir Thomas Gates and the other Bermuda survivors finally reached Jamestown in May 1610, they found the survivors in pitiful condition. As the colony's lieutenant governor, Gates took counsel with the remaining leaders and decided to abandon the settlement. On June 7 the settlers left Jamestown and started down river. Next morning, while en route down the James, Gates received word that Lord De la Warr, the Company-appointed Governor, had arrived at Point Comfort on the way

Everyone worked to build the fort and the various homes and storehouses inside. (From **Pioneers in the Settlement of America** *[1876])*

to Jamestown with 150 settlers and supplies. Gates hastened back to the empty fort and the governor arrived on June 10. The settlement was saved.

(*Editor's note*: A grim reminder of the Starving Time was uncovered at Jamestown in 1956. Skeletons of 70 settlers were by chance dug up on the island near the presumed site of the fort. The shallow graves and absence of caskets indicate hasty burial, probably because survivors had no strength for grave digging.)

This 2007 painting by artist Richard Schlecht shows how the James Fort may have appeared in its early years. (Courtesy of the United States Postal Service)

After Lord De la Warr's arrival, Virginia's course was somewhat smoother. This was chiefly because one of Gates' passengers, John Rolfe, in 1612 introduced the cultivation of Spanish tobacco in Virginia. Work increased, money began to trickle in, new settlers came, and James Fort was deserted for better quarters. A larger church was built outside the fort, and a market square developed around it. New arrivals spread out along the shore to the south of the first houses. Growth was permitted by the peace that followed Rolfe's marriage to Indian Princess Pocahontas in 1614.

This New Town consisted chiefly of houses built along Jamestown's main road much the same way that Englishmen had placed their homes in meandering rows at the crossroads of traffic arteries in the rural farmlands of England. This dusty Great Road gave Virginians the comfortable sense of being in a familiar village, living shoulder-to-shoulder in close contact with neighbors. While row houses were naturally ill lighted, the use of common walls made building easier.

As Jamestown grew, the Great Road that the first settlers developed from James Fort across the isthmus to the mainland was gradually extended. Passing alongside the Glasshouse on the Main, it followed the route of an Indian trail to a point roughly midway between the James and the York rivers where Middle Plantation was cleared. Along this road Governor Sir William Berkeley about 1645 began to build Virginia's first large plantation house, two miles from Jamestown.

Archaeologists both at Jamestown and at Glasshouse Point have identified traces of the Great Road. The route passes close behind the reconstructed Glasshouse of 1608 and the Jamestown Settlement (formerly Jamestown Festival Park.) It is the

This National Park Service diorama in the late 1950s and 1960s depicts the arrival of Lord De la Warr at the James Fort. (Courtesy of the National Park Service, Colonial National Historical Park)

oldest surviving trail in English America.

Jamestown's main residential area always remained close to the fort site. Beyond New Town, the 1,500-acre peninsula dropped off into marsh. Occasional settlers built in clearings on high ground. (Foundations of several such homes are marked along the Wilderness Trail, which the National Park Service developed to guide visitors through the Jamestown woods.)

The spread of tobacco culture after 1612 prompted other settlers to choose farm sites away from Jamestown, on creeks and rivers offering dockage for tobacco ships. For this reason, Governor Sir Thomas Dale began the town of Henricus 40 miles up the James. About the same time, settlements were made at Charles City and at Kecoughtan, which under its later English name, Hampton, is the oldest continuous English-speaking town in America.

It was not long before some of the new settlements were shipping more hogsheads of tobacco than Jamestown. Had it not remained Virginia's capital—contrary to Dale's intentions—Jamestown might have dropped out of sight early in the seventeenth century.

As the center of Virginia's governmental life, however, King James's Town assumed new importance in 1619 with the meeting of the first Virginia General Assembly. Self-government in the new world had been established. Thus, the meeting of the Burgesses and the arrival of the shipload of maids as potential wives in 1620 changed the fortress into a town with a future. Though Virginia remained dangerous and difficult, its settlement was no longer the tragic struggle it had been during the first twelve years, to which so many intrepid Englishmen gave their lives.

From Jamestown, early Virginians could look in any direction and call the land their own. The Virginia Company's charter of 1609 described as Virginia all lands in North American between 34 and 40 degrees latitude, the upper boundary being so tilted as to extend through the Great Lakes and Canada to the Pacific. Near the apex of this triangle sat Jamestown.

The town remained small for the 92 years of its rule as the capital, but its importance grew great. No more than 500 people ever lived in the rude village at one time. Still, it was England's nerve center in the New World.

With the first steps toward home rule in Virginia came also a new sense of permanence. Makeshift shelters were replaced by sturdier homes. Brick and clapboard replaced wattle-and-daub. New houses were made more comfortable by casement windows with green-glass panes. The appalling death rate began to recede slightly.

More family groups debarked from the supply ships, pushing up the James River and its tributaries to claim their headrights on the frontier. Under the headright system, a new settler who paid for his passage was given 50 acres plus another 50 for each person he brought over.

The Indian uprising in March 1622 killed 347 of Virginia's approximately 1,250 settlers and temporarily slowed the burst of settlement. However, Jamestown itself had been forewarned by the friendly Indian youth Chanco and was able to resist, thus preventing even greater carnage.

Jamestown and its related coastline settlements rebounded quickly.

Because Virginia was developing agriculture instead of commerce, the promoters' original conception of four Virginia cities—to be named for King James, the late Queen Elizabeth, Prince Charles, and Prince Henry—failed to materialize. Instead, the newcomers settled along rivers and creeks. By 1627 there were 27 such

A portrait of Thomas West, Lord De la Warr (From the collection of the Jamestown-Yorktown Foundation)

"separate plantations" on mainland Virginia and the Eastern Shore. The census of that year records that 175 people lived at Jamestown, including indentured servants and nine slaves. New Town (on the island outside of the fort) had grown to 33 households along its main road and back street. In all of James City, which included

The settlers were ready to abandon Jamestown when Lord De la Warr arrived with supplies and new colonists. (From a postal card published by the Jamestown Amusement & Vending Co., Norfolk, for the 1907 Jamestown Exposition, courtesy of the editor)

Jamestown and its so-called "suburbs" on the mainland, there were 183 cattle, 265 pigs, 126 goats, and ten boats.

Indeed, so promising did Virginia look that in 1624 King James I, with the help of his Privy Council and attorney general, took its control away from the Virginia Company and made it a royal province. Over the outcries of stockholders, the king thereafter appointed his own royal governor.

The king's representative at Jamestown wielded great power. Not only did he personify the king's authority, but he governed the Anglican Church in the colony, commanded the militia, dealt with the other growing English colonies and the Indians, rewarded supporters with appointments, and presided over the Council.

Act I of the American story had ended. Act II was about to begin. ⚜

The Iron Worker, Spring, 1967, Lynchburg Foundry Company

CHAPTER 9 ❧

Captain John Smith

The father figure at early Jamestown was John Smith. In 1608, about sixteen months after the settlers arrived at Jamestown, the colony's Council after first turning to Edward Maria Wingfield and then John Ratcliffe to serve as president, finally recognized Smith—the most energetic and resourceful of its members.

The choice of Smith gave colonists hope, for he had served as a soldier in Hungary, Turkey, and Transylvania and knew how to survive. He had landed in Virginia in chains, accused of mutiny by Wingfield.

In fact, when the Englishmen set foot first in Virginia at Cape Henry, Smith was not among the group that went ashore. However, when the sealed box of instructions from the London Company was opened, his name was among those to be in leadership posts and his appointment to the Council freed him to explore the tidal creeks and rivers, meeting the Indians and trading for food.

Like most Englishmen of his day, he was no more than five feet tall, but he had a bantam's cockiness. As the least educated member of the Council, he felt obliged to prove himself the equal of the others, and his writings and maps of Virginia and later of New England show him a man of wide knowledge. Handsome and full-bearded, he boasted of his prowess with the ladies but never took a wife.

Portrait of Captain John Smith. (From a nineteenth century copy of the Van de Passe engraving, courtesy of the Collection of the Jamestown-Yorktown Foundation)

Captain John Smith and Indian Princess Pocahontas are intertwined in Jamestown's history. (From a postal card published by the Jamestown Amusement & Vending Co., Norfolk, for the 1907 Jamestown Exposition, courtesy of the editor)

Although Smith shared the Elizabethan taste for boasting, his brisk leadership pumped life into the colony. On one hand he was obliged to satisfy investors, who demanded a search for gold and profitable exports, and on the other the settlers' need for food, shelter, security, and a sense of direction.

Like Raleigh, he was a man of action, imbued with the idea of service to king and country, and like Raleigh he was a skilled writer, sending to England in 1608 a letter that saw publication as *A True Relation* and provided the clearest picture of Virginia until his *Generall Historie of Virginia* was printed in 1624.

In the latter, Smith told of being saved by the lovely Princess Pocahontas (called Matoaka in her native tongue) after he had been condemned to death by Chief Powhatan. The tale delighted endless generations. Many people thought the account was true, but for others it raised endless questions about his veracity.

(*Editor's note*: Pocahontas never married Smith, but wed another settler, John Rolfe, who arrived in Virginia after Smith had departed.)

Author Dennis Montgomery in his study of Smith in the Spring 1994 edition of the *Colonial Williamsburg Journal*, wrote that from Smith's own words "it is difficult to conclude he is due less than a full measure of credit in the founding of the nation. Like many writers of the day, he was not an author to stint on praise of himself, the praise for which his name is enshrined, once in a while in bronze."

After helping the struggling colony survive its first year and welcoming new settlers in January 1608, Smith became president of the Council on September 10, 1608.

Montgomery notes that Smith had been ousted as council president (governor), after just 11 just months on the job, and was succeeded by another of the original settlers, gentleman George Percy, who "wrote that this man Smith was 'an Ambityous unworthy and vayne glorious fellowe.'" Percy's own writings provided another primary source of the settlement.

"After Smith's self aggrandizing books began to gain circulation," Montgomery writes that Percy took exception for the record. Percy wrote, "that many untruths concerning These proceedings have been formerly published wherein The author had not Spared to Appropriate many deserts to himself which he never Performed and stuffed his Relations with so many falsities and malicious detractions..."

Smith was severely injured by a gunpowder explosion in the winter of 1609 and returned to England. His writings spread Virginia's fame and lured settlers who kept Virginia alive.

Smith's contributions to the Jamestown settlement should not be minimized. His persistent and successful travels along the boundaries

The much-debated saving of John Smith by Pocahontas was first revealed by Smith in his book on the Jamestown voyage and early years of the settlement. (From **The Generall Historie of Virginia, New-England and the Summer Isles,** *London [1624], courtesy of the editor)*

of the Chesapeake Bay, up its streams, bays, and rivers, provided a lexicon of Americana for the Englishman back home. In valuable ways, he was a promoter for the colony, encouraging new settlers and describing vast new opportunities in the new land. ⚜

Virginia—The English Heritage in America, Heritage House Publishers, New York, 1966 and notes from an unpublished article, 1995.

CHAPTER 10

John Rolfe and Other Leaders

There were a host of able men among the first settlers to land on the shores of Virginia in 1607. In addition to the well-known Captain John Smith and the voyage-leader, Captain Christopher Newport, there were others, like the Rev. Robert Hunt, a graduate of Oxford University and chaplain to the colony, who faithfully ministered to others until his early death at Jamestown. From Hunt's ministry until the American Revolution, the Church of England (Anglican) was to be a part of Virginia and of America.

Prior to embarking on his mission, Reverend Hunt had served first as Vicar of

No contemporary image exists of John Rolfe, depicted here in a drawing by Sidney E. King. (From the Jamestown-Yorktown Foundation)

Reculver in Kent County (1594–1602) and later as the Vicar of Heatherfield in Sussex County. After landing at Jamestown, he initially held open-air services, according to Capt. John Smith, who described the chaplain as "our honest, religious and courageous divine." When a chapel was erected, Reverend Hunt conducted regular services there and became known throughout the small settlement for his abilities to mediate problems and help resolve confrontations among the settlers. It is believed that he died in the spring of 1608.

The *Godspeed* captain, Bartholomew Gosnold, attended Cambridge University, and was trained as a lawyer, studying at Middle Temple in 1592. The law, however, did not maintain his interest, but the propect of exploring the "New World" did. After first sailing for Sir Walter Raleigh, he later surveyed the New England coast in 1602, discovered and gave the name to "Cape Cod," and gave his daughter's name to Martha's Vineyard, while attempting to create a colony there. In 1606 he became involved with the London Company's efforts to begin a colony in Virginia and was selected to command one of the three ships. Gosnold was one of the Council members named by the Virginia Company in the sealed orders. He was well liked, but his influence was short-lived. He is believed to have died of malaria on August 22, less than four months after arriving at Jamestown, with his burial marked by a firing of "many volleys of small shot" in his honor.

Captain Gabriel Archer, a product of the Inns of Court, was by trade a lawyer, and like his fellow attorney Gosnold, he, too, became infatuated by the exploration urge and sailed with his friend first in 1602 to explore the coast of New England. He probably traveled on board the *Godspeed* with Gosnold when they came to Virginia.

He was among the colonists wounded by the Indians when the colonists first landed, and survived to serve over the first two years at Jamestown in various leadership roles, initially as the colony's recorder (referred to by some as Secretary of State). He was also a member of the Council in 1608. Records indicate that he died in the winter of 1609–1610.

Captain John Martin, son of a three-term Lord Mayor of London, had sailed around the world with Sir Francis Drake and had accompanied Sir Richard Grenville's expedition to relieve the ill-fated Roanoke Island colony. Having survived those early years, Martin took a group of colonists and attempted to plant a settlement in the Nansemond tribal territory, across the James River. Unfortunately, the effort failed, with many of the men dying in the attempt.

Later, he patented Martin's Brandon 20 miles upriver from Jamestown and lived there until his death in 1632, one of the few original settlers to survive the colony's early years. Martin's Plantation was one of those settlements that sent representatives to the first meeting of the House of Burgesses in 1619.

The most nobly born of the settlers was George Percy, the eighth son of the Duke of Northumberland, who entered the military in his youth and served in the Netherlands prior to coming to Virginia. He was a member of the Council from 1607 until he returned to England in April 1612, and during that period also served as president of the Council, governor of Jamestown (1609–1610), and deputy governor (1611).

Percy possessed soldierly qualities and administrative ability, which may account for his orderly records, including a detailed account of the voyage and in-depth letters on many events in early Jamestown history, including the "Starving Time," the winter of 1609 when more than half of the colonists died. Following his return to England in 1612 he returned to military service and later published, "Observations gathered out of a Discourse of the Plantations of the Southern Colonie in Virginia by the English."

Of the original 105 settlers who set out for the New World, one died en route and most of the others died before 1611. Only Robert Beheathland, gentleman, and William Spencer are known to have descendants today.

Another major figure in the early years of the colony was a late arrival, John Rolfe, who distinguished himself on two historical counts: his development and exportation of tobacco to England, and his marriage to the Indian Princess Pocahontas.

Through the years, the celebrated fictional relationship of Pocahontas and John Smith overshadowed the honest romantic quest of Rolfe, who ultimately married the 18-year-old daughter of Chief Powhatan in 1614 in a ceremony witnessed by Governor Thomas Dale, a handful of Pocahontas' people, and the Spanish spy, Molina.

Rolfe arrived in 1609 aboard the *Sea Venture*, the flagship of a nine-ship relief/supply fleet, carrying 500 new settlers. The voyage was made more difficult by an encounter with a hurricane off Bermuda, where the ships were forced in for repairs. There, Rolfe's daughter was born and christened Bermuda. She died very soon afterwards and his wife apparently died shortly after arriving at Jamestown.

In 1610 John Rolfe began experimenting with tobacco and is credited with raising the first non-native tobacco in Virginia. A year or so later, Pocahontas was kidnapped and carried to Jamestown to be traded for English prisoners the Indians had captured. But the prisoner exchange never materialized, and Pocahontas was moved to the settlement at Henrico, upriver from Jamestown, where she learned the English

About a year after her conversion to Christianity, Pocahontas married John Rolfe, who arrived in Jamestown in 1610. (From a postal card published by the Jamestown Amusement & Vending Co., Norfolk, for the 1907 Jamestown Exposition, courtesy of the editor)

language and was baptized a Christian. About this time Rolfe met the Indian maid and fell in love with her.

Historians note that Rolfe was a pious man, who wrote to Thomas Dale, governor of the Colony, asking for permission to marry her. Rolfe wrote, "It is Pocahontas to whom my hearty and best thoughts are, and have been a long time so entangled, and enthralled in so intricate a labyrinth that I (could not) unwind myself thereout." They were married in the spring of 1614 bringing a temporary peace between the natives and colonists.

Rolfe and his wife and infant son, Thomas, later traveled to England where they were celebrated and feted and where Pocahontas was presented at the court of King James I. Unfortunately for Rolfe and ultimately

This famous engraving of Matoaka, Pocahontas' Indian name, apparently was done in England during her visit. (From **The Generall Historie of Virginia, New-England and the Summer Isles**, *London [1624], courtesy of the editor)*

the colony, Pocahontas died at Gravesend, England, at the beginning of their homeward journey to Virginia. Rolfe decided to leave Thomas in England with a guardian when he returned to the colony to reassume his prominent role. From 1614–1619, he served as a member of Council and as the "Secretary of State."

Later he was married to Jane Pearce, daughter of a colonist, and continued his active work with tobacco. Thomas was still in England in 1622 when Rolfe, ironically, fell victim to the massacre of the colonists by the Indians. Thomas lived to perpetuate a Virginia family second in age in English America only to the family lines left by Beheathland and Spencer. ✾

Virginia—The English Heritage in America, Hastings House Publishers, New York, 1966

CHAPTER 11 ❧

Life Among the Powhatans

Werowocomoco, the capital of the Powhatan "empire," was the favorite town of the principal chief, Powhatan. Located on the York River in the present Gloucester County, when Jamestown was first settled, it was there that John Smith visited the chief in 1608 and found him "a tall well proportioned man, with a sower look, his head somewhat gray, his beard so thinne, that is seemeth none at all, his age neare sixtie; of a very able and hardy body to endure any labour."

In 1609 Powhatan moved his quarters to Orapaks in western New Kent County to be farther removed from Jamestown, and there he ruled until his death in 1618.

Interpreters Doris and James Ware of the Rappahannock tribe stand in a dance circle of the recon-structed Powhatan Indian village in the late 1950s at Jamestown Festival Park, now Jamestown Settlement. (From the collection of the Jamestown-Yorktown Foundation)

By the year 1600, Indian life in Virginia had lost much of its nomadic quality. With the development of agriculture, tribal hunters went out from town to get food—fish and game, rather than roaming. Villages had become permanent, and palisades were often built around those near enemy territory. These and other aspects of Virginia Indian life were similar to the Indians of Roanoke Island, North Carolina, and probably similar to the familiar paintings by John White in 1584–86

The title of this engraving is "Chickahominies Become New Englishmen." (From Theodor de Bry, America, *Part XIV [1630], courtesy of the Jamestown-Yorktown Foundation)*

of other Indians in the Carolina sounds area. Lodges or wigwams were built of saplings set in the ground in circular or rectangular fashion, bent and tied together at the top, and covered with bark or mats of reeds and grasses. A wide hurdle, or shelf, around the interior of the lodge provided bed space, and a fire in the center of the floor sent up its smoke through a hole in the roof.

William Strachey, one of the original Jamestown settlers, wrote: "As for their howses, who knoweth one of them knoweth them all, even the Chief kings house it self, for they be all alike builded one to another, they are like gardein arbours, (at best like our shepherd cottages,) made yet handsomely enough, though without strength or gaynes [notches], of such young plants as they can pluck up, goe, and make the greene toppes meete together in fashion of a round roofe, which they thatch with mattes, throwne over, the walls are made with barkes of trees, but then those be principall howses, for so many barkes which doe to the making up of a howse, are long type of purchasing, in the midst of the howse there is a lover [louver], out of which the smoake yssueth, the fire being kept right under, every howse commonly hath twoo doores, one before and a Postern, the doores be hung with matts, never locked nor bolted, but only those matts be to turne up, or let fall at pleasure."

Around their villages the Powhatan Indians grew pumpkins, beans, gourds, and tobacco in plots cleared with stone axes and fire. "Their houses," wrote Smith, "are in the midst of their fields or gardens, which are small plots of ground. Some 20 acres, some 40, some 100, some 200, some more, some lesse." He adds: "To prepare

Indians burned out a log and carefully scraped the inside for their canoe. (Engraved by Theodor de Bry in 1590 from Thomas Hariot's Admiranda Narratio fida tamen, de Commodis et Incolarum Ritibus Virginiae, *Frankfurt, [1590])*

the ground they bruise the barke of the trees neare the root, they scortch the roots with fire that they grow no more. The next yeare with a crooked piece of wood they beat up the weeds by the rootes, and in that mould they plant their corne. Their manner is this. They make a hole in the earth with a stick, and into it they put foure graines of wheate and two of beanes..."

As in other primitive societies, much heavy work was allotted to women. Continues Smith, "The men bestow their times in fishing, hunting, warres, and such man-like exercise, scorning to be seene in any woman-like exercise, which is the cause that the women be very painefull, and the men often idle. The women and the children doe the rest of the worke. They make mats, baskets, pots, mortars, pound their corne, make their bread, prepare their victuals, plant their corne, gather their corne, beare all kind of burdens, and such like."

As with their houses, the Powhatan Indians followed the mode of dress shown by John White in his Roanoke Island paintings. Their clothes are described again by Smith:

"They are some time covered with the skinnes of wilde beasts, which in winter are dressed with the hayre, but in sommer without. The better sort use large mantels of deare skins, not much different in fashion with the Irish mantels. Some inbrodered with white beads, some with copper, other painted after their manner. But the common sort have scarce to cover their nakednesse, but with grasse, the leaves of trees, or such like. We have seene some use mantels of Turky feathers, so prettily wrought and woven with threads that nothing could be discerned but the feathers. That was exceeding warm and very handsome. But the women are always covered about their middles with a skin, and very shamefast to be seene bare."

The bow and arrow remained the chief Indian weapon in the seventeenth century. The Indians, however, did learn to use firearms beginning in 1616–1617 and managed to get hold of arms and ammunition thereafter in spite of English efforts. The passing of laws forbidding the sale of firearms to the Indians from 1618 onward indicates that sales were constant. And their crafts continued despite spasmodic trading of English beads, trinkets, or articles of clothing for Indian corn, tobacco, or wild game. Very skeptically, the Europeans in Virginia and the Indians tried to co-exist peaceably. Englishmen learned from Indians how to hollow logs for boats, to trap animals and net fish, to plant beans and tobacco, and to grind corn into meal. The Indians, for their part, learned English words, copied English methods of soil cultivation, and eventually acquired English firearms. But culturally they remained miles apart.

Powhatan's tribesmen were handsome people. Inured to cold, they wore animal

This may be the dish described by Captain John Smith in his Generall Historie: *"In winter they esteem it (corn) being boyled with beanes for a rare fish they call Pausarowmena." (Engraved by Theodor de Bry in 1590 from Thomas Hariot's* Admiranda Narratio fida tamen, de Commodis et Incolarum Ritibus Virginiae, *Frankfurt, [1590])*

skins in winter and summer. Chiefs and priests had deerskin mantles embroidered with white beads or copper, or painted bright colors. The higher one's rank, the more he wore.

To toughen boys for a warrior's life, they were isolated in the woods for a period of nine months between the ages of ten and fifteen. During this ordeal they were not permitted to speak. Tribal leaders taught them religious lore and some became "priests and conjurers." The practice was similar to the "husquenawing" followed by the Siouan-speaking tribesmen south of Virginia and described by John Lawson a century later:

"...Most commonly, once a year, at farthest, once in two years, these people take up so many of their young men as they think are able to undergo it and husquenaugh them, which is to make them obedient and respective to their superiors, and, as they say, is the same to them as it is to us to send our children to school, to be taught good breeding and letters. This house of correction is a large, strong cabin, made on purpose for the reception of the young men and boys that have not passed the graduation already; and it is always at Christmas that they husquenaugh their youth, which is by bringing them into this house and keeping them dark all the time, where they more than half starve them.

"Besides, they give the pellitory bark, and several intoxicating plants, that make them go raving mad as ever were any people in the world; and you may hear them make the most dismal and hellish cries and howlings that ever human creatures expressed; all which continues about five or six weeks...

Mike Krigsvold, a Pamunkey Indian from King William County, prepares deer skin by removing hair with a stone at the Powhatan Indian site at Jamestown Festival Park, now Jamestown Settlement. (from the Newport News **Daily Press,** *photo by Herb Barnes)*

The Indians planted corn and beans regularly near all of their villages. (Engraved by Theodor de Bry in 1590 from Thomas Hariot's Admiranda Narratio fida tamen, de Commodis et Incolarum Ritibus Virginiae, *Frankfurt, [1590])*

"Now, when they first come out, they are as poor as ever any creatures were; for you must know several die under the diabolical purgation. Moreover, they either really are, or pretend to be, dumb, and do not speak for several days; I think twenty or thirty, and look so ghastly and are so changed that it is next to an impossibility to know them again, although you were ever so well acquainted with them before...

"...Now the savages say if it were not for this they could never keep their youth in subjection; besides that, it hardens them ever after to the fatigues of war, hunting, and all manner of hardship, which their way of life exposes them to. Beside, they add that it carries off those infirm, weak bodies that would have been only a burden and disgrace to their nation and saves the victuals and clothing for better people than would have been expended on such unless creatures."

Despite English efforts to coexist peaceably, the Powhatans were resentful of the intruders. Hostages were traded as insurance against attack, but both peoples committed wanton cruelties.

*The colonists found natives playful but dangerous. From a watercolor
by John White. (Engraved by Theodor de Bry in 1590 from Thomas
Hariot's* **Admiranda Narratio fida tamen, de Commodis et
Incolarum Ritibus Virginiae,** *Frankfurt, [1590])*

(*Editor's note*: In 2003 archaeologists from the Virginia Department of Historic Resources [VDHR] and the College of William and Mary believed that they had found Chief Powhatan's headquarters on Purton Bay overlooking the York River in Gloucester County.

Randolph Turner III, Portsmouth Regional Director of VDHR, explained that everything seems to put Werowocomoco at this location. The *Gloucester Mathews-Gazette Journal* reported, "Maps from the early settlement period indicated that Powhatan's headquarters were in that vicinity," Turner said. "English colonists described a site on a bay fed by three creeks, conforming to Purton Bay. Distances match those described by the English, and a site near Timberneck advocated by some as Werowocomoco do not." Nearby springs provide fresh water, the soil is excellent for farming, and the high site commands a broad view of friends and enemies who would arrive by water, Turner explained in the newspaper.

Excavations already have revealed outlines of a village. The site also has yielded hundreds of pottery and stone artifacts consistent with Indian occupation.) ⚜

The Iron Worker, Summer 1965, Lynchburg Foundry Company

CHAPTER 12 ❧

The Search for Gold

The chief object of Virginia's settlement was to find the "treasure" that England needed to build ships and to pay armies, as Spain had done. In the Virginia charter of 1606, it was specified that a fifth of the gold and silver found should belong to the King, with the rest going to the London Company and its founders. Settlers scoured the Tidewater earth, but the supposed ore they sent by Christopher Newport's second return voyage in 1608 proved to be only fool's gold.

No better luck rewarded their second objective—to find a water course westward through North America and thence to Cipangu (Japan) and Cathay (China). This had been reported by Ralph Lane and quoted in Hakluyt's *Voyages* published in 1599. Captain Newport in 1607 sailed his three ships as far up Virginia's westernmost river as he could, but the fall line forced him back to Jamestown.

Undaunted, John Smith probed each creek and river for the next two years, but no westward passage materialized. To England's dismay, the Dutch and Portuguese continued to drain off the gold of the East Indies unchallenged.

"Gold fever" so seduced the minds of most early settlers that Jamestown nearly died for lack of food. It led the gentlemen adventurers who made up half of the settlement to spend their energy in fruitless search instead of fishing or raising crops.

Except for a few realists like Smith, John Rolfe, and Sir Thomas

A conjectural illustration of the interior of the colonists' glasshouse at Jamestown. (From A Tryal of Glasse—The Story of Glassmaking at Jamestown, *courtesy of Eastern National)*

England's honest and industrious yeoman farmers were actively recruited by the London Company to become settlers at Jamestown. (From Marshall W. Fishwick, Jamestown, First English Colony *[1965])*

Dale, Jamestown would have died of starvation. The effect on Virginia Company investors was quickly demoralizing. The Spanish ambassador in London reported to his government that "This plantation has lost much ground, as it was sustained by companies of merchants, who were disappointed at finding no gold nor other silver mines, nor the passage to the South Sea which they had hoped for."

Fortunately, England needed other raw materials abounding in Virginia. Timbers for ships' masts were sent back by the returning *Susan Constant* and *Godspeed*, and lumber thereafter remained an important export throughout Virginia's history. True, the colony was not able to supply the olive oil, citrus fruits, and wine that the Bristol merchant William Parkhurst had glowingly predicted in 1582. Neither could it produce the salt, sugar, grains, and hides that Spain was importing from her Latin American colonies; nor the exotic spices, porcelain, Japan work, and lacquer that Portugal and the Netherlands were extracting from the Indies.

England also wanted her own supply of glass and raw materials—tar pitch, timber, and soap ashes—that the Muscovy Company had imported from Russia and Poland. Virginia could and did produce these. Glass was first blown here in 1608, and such staples as wheat, Indian corn, barrels, boats, and pitch and tar for caulking hulls and tarring rigging were produced.

Besides its desire for gold, the Virginia Company hoped to produce certain luxury goods in Virginia to compete with the Orient's. Most of England's wealth was in the hands of city merchants and nobles, who passionately desired the exotic imports from China and Japan. Luxury goods for this class were highly saleable, for it had "ready money." The Virginia Company encouraged settlers to produce them. Wrote the poet James Cathorne in his *Essays on Taste*: "Of late, 'tis true, quite sick of Rome and Greece, We fetch our models from the wise Chinese."

For the luxury trade, Virginia made trial from 1608 to 1620 of various commodities. When Captain George Yeardley arrived in Virginia in 1618 as deputy governor, he was directed by the company to promote the growing of flax to make linen. However, the plant did not take to Virginia's soil, and the effort was abandoned. More desirable still was silk, which was in high fashion in Europe. English promoters believed silkworms would flourish in Virginia's climate, and mulberry trees were planted at Jamestown to feed them. King James himself encouraged this project in the desire to supply European silk weavers who set up silk manufactures in 1608 at Spitalfields and Morefields, near London.

As Virginia's first Assembly in 1619, the House of Burgesses enacted into law a Virginia Company proposal that each settler plant six mulberry trees for seven years. Instructions for growing mulberry leaves and feeding the silkworms were prepared for the colony by the head of the Royal Silk Establishment, and an expert grower was sent to Jamestown with a supply of worms from Spain and Italy. Some silk fibre was returned to England, but the infant industry was destroyed in the uprising of 1622.

Shown here are some of the methods of farming in England practiced by Virginia's settlers. (From Johann Amos Comenius, Orbis Sensualis *[1658])*

The smuggling into Virginia of Spanish-type tobacco seed from Trinidad in 1612 saved the colony's economy. (From a Sidney E. King painting, courtesy of the National Park Service, Colonial National Historical Park)

Another luxury product that the company encouraged was wine. Since the Norman Conquest in 1066, Englishmen had fancied European wines, but wars and customs duties limited the supply. In all Europe only Portugal, which was usually allied with England against France and Spain, was a dependable supplier. The Portuguese vintners' sherry, port, and madeira became English standbys. Nevertheless, England tried to reproduce French and Italian vintages for 300 years in her colonies. Virginia's native scuppernong and fox grapes were pressed and fermented from 1609 onward, but English gourmets were not enthusiastic.

Wine making was endorsed in 1619, in the deliberations of the first Virginia Assembly at Jamestown. The Virginia Company in that year sent French growers to Jamestown with grape rootings from Languedoc, but settlers derided both the workmen and their efforts. The wine that they sent back to London and Bristol was so poor that they were accused of sabotage. After the 1622 Indian uprising, the neglected vineyards were spoiled by deer. Wine making was often tried in later years, but with little success. ⚜

Planters and Pioneers:—Life in Colonial Virginia, Hastings House Publishers, New York 1970

CHAPTER 13 ✤

The Colony Grows

Virginia grew. Settlers dared to move out of James Fort, building homes along Jamestown's paths or on the banks of neighboring creeks. Jamestown became a village of narrow wooden row houses following the meandering course of its cart roads. By 1612 the colony had reached a population of 800, most of them men, and another settlement was beginning at Kecoughtan, near the guns of Fort Algernon, in the present-day city of Hampton.

Governor Sir Thomas Dale saw the need for a capital farther up the James, and selected a peninsula at Dutch Gap, near the present Richmond. There he had settlers build a new palisade, a blockhouse, and homes to accommodate 300 persons, calling it Henricus to honor King James' son, Prince Henry. A University of Henrico was proposed, and the Virginia Company pledged 10,000 acres for its use. The industrious Dale also founded other settlements farther westward on the James at Bermuda Hundred and Shirley Hundred.

Peace with the Indians encouraged this growth. John Rolfe married Pocahontas in 1614, and the effect of his union might have fostered a permanent peace had not Pocahontas died three years later at Gravesend, England,

Books and broadsides were frequently published in England about the emerging Jamestown settlement in Virginia. This book was printed at Oxford. (From Robert Jonson, Nova Britannia, *Oxford [1609])*

The Virginia Company in 1615 conducted a lottery to raise funds for the settlement. (From the Society of Antiquarians of London)

while returning with Rolfe and their infant son Thomas, after presentation at the English court. A year after her untimely death, the aged Powhatan himself died, transferring power over the Indians to the aggressive Chief Opechancanough.

The military rule of Jamestown's early years violated the promise of full British rights to the settlers, and resentment developed as the colony gained strength. Some Virginia Company officials were sympathetic, and these took advantage of conflict among the stockholders to gain power and make changes. Sir Thomas Smythe, who had headed the company, was blamed for early disappointments. In 1612 dissatisfied stockholders amended the company charter to give his office less power and them-selves more by having more frequent company meetings.

Smythe and his fellow London businessmen, who because of their closeness to the King were known as the Court Party, thus came into conflict with stock-holders outside London, known as the Country Party. A quarrel broke out between Smythe and Lord Rich, afterward the Earl of Warwick. In 1618 Warwick and his Country Party adherents replaced Smythe as treasurer with Sir Edwin Sandys, a liberal member of Parliament from rural England.

Under Sandys' leadership, the London Company began to move toward self-government in Virginia. At its quarterly "court" on November 28, 1618, it ratified a more democratic order in The Great Charter of Privileges, Orders, and Laws and dispatched Governor Sir George Yeardley to Jamestown with instructions to con-vene a General Assembly.

In response to Yeardley's call, an election was duly held, and two Burgesses from each of the eleven principal localities in Virginia gathered at Jamestown on July 30, 1619, and met in the choir stalls of the new wooden church outside the deserted remains of James Fort. This was the first legislative body to meet in the New World. For the next 150 years it was to try valiantly to obtain for colonists in Virginia the rights that they believed due every Englishman wherever he might live. In seeking such rights, Virginia's Assemblymen were joining an evolutionary movement that had been under way in England for 400 years, gradually circum

scribing the powers of king and nobles, while enlarging the rights of the common man. The eventual revolt of Virginia and the other American colonies occurred because neither King nor Parliament would concede to colonists the rights of native Englishmen.

The beginning of Virginia's political life in 1619 was made possible by the infusion of strength from tobacco cultivation. While self-government was to come slowly, Sandys was wise enough to see that England in Virginia demanded some measure of political growth if it was to thrive. Under Sandys' leadership, the Company in 1619 further stimulated Virginians' permanence and ambition by awarding a grant of land to each settler. "Ancient planters" who had come in the first nine years each received 100 acres, while subsequent arrivals received 50 acres plus an additional 50 for each person brought over. Another practical step was the dispatch by the Company of a shipload of young women, or "maids" to become wives for settlers who paid for their

THE
PROCEEDINGS OF
THE ENGLISH COLONIE IN
Virginia fince their firft beginning from England in the yeare of our Lord 1606, till this prefent 1612, with all their accidents that befell them in their Iournies and Difcoveries.

Alfo the Salvages difcourfes, orations and relations of the Bordering neighbours, and how they became fubiect to the Englifh.

Vnfolding even the fundamentall caufes from whence haue fprang fo many miferies to the vndertakers, and fcandals to the bufineffe: taken faithfully as they were, written out of the writings of Thomas Studley the firft prouant maifter, Anas Todkill, Walter Ruffell Doctor of Phificke, Nathaniell Powell, William Phettyplace, Richard Wiffin, Thomas Abbay, Tho: Hope, Rich: Potts and the labours of divers other diligent obferuers, that were refidents in Virginia.

And peruſed and confirmed by diverfe now refident in England that were actors in this bufines.
By W. S.

AT OXFORD,
Printed by Jofeph Barnes. **1612.**

A broadside about the first years at Jamestown was printed in London in 1609 and sold by Samuel Machem at his shop in St. Paul's church-yard, at the sign of the bulhead. (From the Rouse Collection at the Earl Gregg Swem Library, College of William and Mary)

THE
NEW LIFE
of Virginea:
DECLARING THE
FORMER SVCCESSE AND PREfent eftate of that plantation, being the fecond part of *Nova Britannia*.

Publifhed by the authoritie of his Maiefties Counfell of *Virginea*.

LONDON,
Imprinted by *Felix Kyngfton* for *William Welby*, dwelling at the figne of the Swan in Pauls Churchyard. 1612.

The broadside entitled The New Life of Virginia *described the progress in the often-embattled colony. (From the Virginia Historical Society)*

transportation. A few women had preceded them to Jamestown, beginning with the arrival in 1608 of a Mrs. Forrest and her maid. ❧

Virginia—The English Heritage in America, Hastings House Publishers, New York, 1966

CHAPTER 14 ✤

Jamestown Medicine Was Gory

A mong the most graphic moments in the highly acclaimed Ken Burns' Public Broadcasting System television documentary, "The Civil War," are those devoted to the crude medical treatment of casualties. Today's sophisticated medicine is a far cry from that known to Federal and Confederate physicians.

But Civil War medicine was infinitely better than that which had been practiced in eighteenth-century Williamsburg. Similarly, the medical practice of Thomas Jefferson's day was a vast improvement over that at Jamestown in 1607, even though two "chirurgions," or surgeons [William Wilkinson and Gentleman Thomas Wotton] were among the 104 settlers who came ashore there to plant English civilization in North America.

The human body and its functions were largely a mystery to Europeans of

Doctor Laurence Bohum experimented with herbs at Jamestown in 1610. (From a Sidney E. King sketch, courtesy of the National Park Service, Colonial National Historical Park)

Costumed interpreters at Jamestown Festival Park in the late 1950s demonstrate seventeenth-century herbal treatment for illness in a building at the reconstructed James Fort. (From the collection of the Jamestown-Yorktown Foundation)

Jamestown's day. Their *Humoral Dictionary* taught them, mistakenly, that nature was made up of four elements: earth, wind, fire and water. In humans, these were thought to take the form of blood, phlegm, black bile, and yellow bile.

The seventeenth-century "doctors" believed that the imbalances between these "humors" caused all diseases. If too much or too little of a "humor" beset the human body, they concluded, illness would result.

To restore the body's balance, Jamestown surgeons resorted to bleeding, purging, or "puking" the patient. Many patients died from the mistaken belief that drawing off "excessive" blood would relieve some ailments. Less fatal was the seventeenth-century belief in frequent emetics to promote vomiting, cathartics to promote excretion, and diuretics to promote urination.

Not until 1628 did England's Sir William Harvey publish his theory of the circulation of blood and the heart's role as its pump. Later in the mid-eighteenth century, the Scottish physician John Hunter revealed the mysteries of the human anatomy, and his English contemporary Edward Jenner discovered inoculation against smallpox.

Colonists were constantly in search of the right herbs for medical use. (From a Sidney E. King paint-ing, courtesy of the National Park Service, Colonial National Historical Park)

In Jamestown's day, barbers also served as primitive surgeons. A barber, Thomas Couper, also was among the first 1607 settlers. Medical progress was seriously hampered in those days by the refusal of physicians to perform surgery. Whiskey was used to deaden the patient's suffering from pain. Although the germ theory of disease was unknown at Jamestown, settlers knew that some illness stemmed from sewage and human filth.

Part of the martial law in 1611 made it illegal to dump waste-water in the streets or to wash within 40 feet of any well or pump. It declared "Nor shall any one within less than a quarter mile from the Palisades [James Fort] dare to do the necessities of nature, since… the whole fort may be choked and poisoned with ill airs."

George Percy's *Account of the Voyage to Virginia and the Colony's First Days* is the first mention of disease and illness at Jamestown. He records the death of two men on August 15, 1607; one on the 16th; one on the 17th; two on the 18th; one on the 19th; and Captain Bartholomew Gosnold, a member of Council, on the 22nd. Five more men died before the end of the month.

Percy writes, "Our men were destroyed with cruell diseases as Swellings, Fluxes, burning Fevers, and by warres, and some departed suddenly…There were never Englishmen left in a forreigne Countrey in such miserie as wee were in this new discovered Virginia."

What became of the two surgeons Wilkinson and Wotton in the first group of settlers is not readily known, but two apothecaries—Thomas Field and John Harford—and another "Chirurgion," Post Ginnat, arrived in the first supply by Captain Christopher Newport on January 2, 1608. A "doctor" John Pott "was appointed in 1621 physician to the colony on the recommendation of the distinguished physician Gulstone, who spoke of him as 'a Master of Arts and well practiced in Chirurgerie and physique,'" according to Lyon G. Tyler's *The Cradle of the Republic—Jamestown and James River*, published in 1906.

(*Editor's note:* The earliest known evidence of surgery and autopsy in the early seventeenth-century was found after forensic analysis of a small piece of human skull discovered by archaeologists in a 400-year-old trash pit at the Jamestown site.

Dr. William M. Kelso, director of archaeology for APVA Preservation Virginia, who began working on the "Jamestown Rediscovery" project in the mid-1990's, made the announcement in December 2004.

Kelso said the hand-size fragment of bone, about four inches by four and three-quarters inches, was found in a bulwark trench surrounding the west corner of the James fort site and apparently had been discarded there with other trash no later than 1610, based upon other artifacts found in the same context. No other bones related to the person were recovered. "It appears to have been discarded as medical waste," Kelso explained.

"Dr. Douglas W. Owsley, forensic osteologist at the National Museum of Natural History, Smithsonian Institution, and Dr. Ashley H. McKeown, forensic anthropologist at the University of Montana, believe that it was a piece of occipital bone from the back of the skull of a European man. This individual received a traumatic blow to the back of his head with a celt-like object, like an axe made of stone, that fratured his skull," the APVA news release said.

"Circular cut marks in the bone show that a surgeon attempted to drill two holes in the skull using a trepan to relieve pressure. [The procedure was not completed] probably because the patient died. Saw marks on the top edge of the bone indicate that an autopsy was subsequently performed."

The APVA also reported that archaeologists have unearthed medical tools and objects at the James Fort site including a *Spatula mundane*, part of a bullet extractor and numerous pieces of pottery from apothecary jars, which typically were used to hold herbs and medicines.) ⚜

Newport News *Daily Press*, March 31, 1991

CHAPTER 15

Early Virginia Wives— a Varied Group

It was a big day at Jamestown when three supply ships arrived in 1619 from England bearing 57 women from London to become wives of settlers. Little has been known by historians of those venturesome ladies until the mid-1980s when a list of their names and native towns was found in the library of Magdalene College at Cambridge University in England.

Now the updated story of those "Wives for Virginia, 1619" is told from the Cambridge papers in the summer 1991 edition of the *William and Mary Quarterly*.

The Virginia Company hoped women of many social ranks would eventually go to Virginia. (From John Speed, Theatrum Imperii Magnae Britanniae [1676])

Historian David Ransome writes interestingly about the women, who range in age from 15 to 28 and in social status from plain to fancy. They were a varied group.

Records of early Virginia hitherto told little about the 57 women except that they were claimed as wives by bachelors or widowers on their arrival. And almost certainly, many of them were among the 300 settlers killed by Indians the next year in the uprising against the James River settlements.

The "maids" were sent to Virginia by the Virginia Company of London to permit marriage and ensure continuity for the Jamestown pioneers. Unlike Spain's Central American settlers, England's overseas adventurers were discouraged by British policy from marrying native women. John Rolfe's marriage to Pocahontas was a rare exception.

The Magdalene College lists speaks of "sending of young, handsome, and honestlie educated Maides to Virginia: There to be disposed in Marriage to the most honest and industrious planters..." who were each required to pay 150 pounds of the

A nineteenth-century engraving suggests the young maidens arriving at Jamestown in 1619. (From the editor's collection)

best leaf tobacco for a bride. Dissatisfaction understandably developed among poor planters at Jamestown who could not afford a wife.

Several well-known English officials invested money in sending the women, in hopes of profit. The chief one was the Earl of Southampton, who invested 48 pounds. Sir Edwin Sandys, the wealthy Londoner who headed the Virginia Company, put in 40 pounds. John and Nicholas Ferrar, who were also the backers of the Virginia Company, also subscribed heavily. It is from their papers in Magdalene College that the new information about the 1621 shipment of women was found.

Nicholas Ferrar listed most of the women sent to Virginia that year aboard the ships *Marmaduke*, *Warwick* and *Tiger*. They included such typically English names as Lettice King, Joane Haynes, Anne Richards, Elizabeth Grinbey, Allice Burges, Allice Goughe, Ann Tanner, and Allice Grove.

Writes historian Ransome from the Rhode Island School of Design, "Of the 57 women who sailed, the ages of 51 are given, ranging from 28 to 15 or 16. Three were widows...Eleven were described as 'maids,' and presumably the others were also...The baby of the 57 was Jane Dier, who was said to be 15 or 16."

About a third of the women came from London. Eight of them, surprisingly, had links with the English gentry, who ranked just below the nobility in the English hierarchy. Four were described as daughters of "gentlefolk," while three others had relatives who were knights, prefixing their names with "Sir." Six of the 57 had male relatives already in Virginia or accompanying them on the three 1621 ships.

But Ransome points out many of the women lacked a "natural defender"—a parent who might otherwise have helped them in England. Writes the author, "In only five families is it certain that both parents were still alive, but there is a possibility that the same was true for another six."

There were 57 women who arrived in 1619 searching for possible husbands in Virginia. (From a postal card published by the Jamestown Amusement and Vending Co., Norfolk, for the 1907 Jamestown Exposition, courtesy of the editor)

Little is told in the Ferrar papers of the housekeeping skills of the 57 women, except for the endorsements of a few family members or former employers. Kinfolk vouched for seven women and a former master or mistress vouched for eight others.

Allice Burges, one of the maids, was described as "skillful in anie countrie work. She can brue, bake, and make malte & c." Ann Tanner, who was 26 or 27, was not only "of honest conversacion" but could "Spinn and sewe in blackworke...brue, and bake, make butter and cheese, and doe huswifery."

The three ships bearing the women sailed for Virginia from the Isle of Wight, and the cost of the passage was calculated at six pounds. The ships reached Jamestown just before Christmas 1621, and the women were soon courted and proposed to by settlers. When the three ships left Jamestown in the spring of 1622, many of the 57 women had been married.

In conclusion, Ransome asks: "What happened to them thereafter? Unless they were especially lucky...all too few of them were still alive in the summer of 1623. Those who survived the Indian attack in March 1622 were likely to have succumbed in the starving winter of 1622–23." Ransome feels sure that the Indians in the 1622 uprising killed Cicely Bray and Marie Daucks, and he fears for at least five others. Still, many survived, to leave descendants in the nation today.

Author Ransome is impressed by the variety of background of these and other primitive Virginia adventurers. He writes, "Alongside criminals and waifs from the streets of London were women from a noticeably different level of society, daughters of the gentry or of artisans and tradesmen." From such simple beginnings Virginia eventually grew. ⚜

Newport News *Daily Press*, June 16, 1991

CHAPTER 16 ✤

Tobacco: Honey-Colored Money

A product that was infinitely better suited than mining or manufacturing to the colony's rich soil and its limited labor supply finally gratified England's economic ambitions in Virginia. This was tobacco.

First having been known to Europeans during Columbus' discovery of the West Indies in 1492, it had in the next hundred years spread through fashionable circles on the continent. Its introduction in the court of Queen Elizabeth I was credited to Sir Walter Raleigh and to Ralph Lane, his colleague in the ill-fated Roanoke Island settlement in North Carolina in 1584. By the time Virginia was settled, pipe smoking had become a mark of urbanity, and tobacco shops had sprung up in England's port towns.

Offended by tobacco smoke and its taste, effete King James I tried to discourage the "stinking weed." He declared it "loathsome to the eye, hateful to the nose, harmful to the brain [and] dangerous to the lungs." In a proclamation in 1604 he imposed a fine on users, complaining that "by immoderate taking of tobacco the health of a great number of our peo-

John Rolfe planted the first tobacco crop in Virginia in 1612 as depicted in this Sidney E. King painting. Indian maid Pocahontas is seated in the foreground, and the James Fort is in the rear. (From the collection of the Jamestown-Yorktown Foundation)

ple is impaired, and their bodies weakened and made unfit for labor." However, many Englishmen continued to consider it a cure for all ailments. One described it as an "antidote to all poisons; that it expelled rheums, sour humors, and obstructions of all kinds, and healed wounds better than St. John's wort." Even apothecaries sold it and demonstrated its use.

In the early seventeenth century, tobacco leaves were spun on spinning wheels into thin ropes, which were coiled into acorn-shaped mounds for convenient sale to pipe smokers. Pictures of coiled tobacco and slaves were shown on English tobacconists' signs and on printed tobacco labels to signify Virginia tobacco after 1620.

Virginia's settlers found the Indians smoked tobacco, but it was far less palatable than the Spanish product. The shipments of Indian leaf they sent to London and Bristol accordingly found few buyers until 1612 when John Rolfe obtained seeds of the Spanish leaf and grew the first saleable crop in Virginia. Where and how Rolfe obtained the seed is unknown, for Spain prohibited its sale; perhaps it was from Don Fernando de Berrio, governor of Trinidad, who in 1612 was fined for "trading with the enemy." All that is known certainly is that William Strachey, the colony's secretary, recorded in 1612 that Rolfe's seeds came from Trinidad, then a

An old engraving of a tobacco plant. (From E. R. Billings, Tobacco, its History, Varieties, Culture... *)*

Spanish possession. Presumably a Dutch or English seaman had smuggled them thence to Jamestown.

Rolfe's Spanish tobacco was the desirable large-leaf variety known as *Nicotiana tabacum,* from which the modern tobacco plant has evolved. Its growth had originated in pre-Columbian South America and spread by trade between prehistoric Indian tribes. Cultivation of this variety by 1492 had reached the West Indies, where Columbus discovered it. Meanwhile, a smaller-leafed tobacco, called *Nicotiana rustica,* had spread by 1607 over a much wider area, reaching as far northward as the present New Brunswick. This was a bitter-tasting leaf grown by the Indians when

Virginia was settled. The area of its cultivation through the New World was almost identical to that of corn, another South American plant that had been spread by Indian trade.

Rolfe's shipment late in 1612 or 1613 changed England's reaction to the Virginia leaf. Here at last was good news from Virginia, for England had been buying tobacco from Spain and worsening her trade balance. In 1615 some 2,300 pounds of tobacco were shipped out from Virginia, and the following year 20,000 pounds were exported. Thereafter, except during the Indian uprisings in 1622 and 1644, the crop grew in size almost yearly until the European market was denied to Virginia by England's Navigation Act of 1651. This and subsequent Acts in 1660 and 1663 caused a decline in price from four-pence a pound in 1650 to halfpenny in 1667, but even at this low price, plantations with slave labor could make a profit.

Tobacco culture set the pattern for life in lowland Virginia from Jamestown in 1613 to the great river-fronted plantations in antebellum Virginia 250 years later. The Virginia Company's early vision of farms and cottage industries clustering around the ports of Jamestown, Kecoughtan, York, and Norfolk—in James City, Charles City, and Elizabeth City—vanished as settlers claimed their 50 acres (100 for those who came before 1616) on creeks and rivers and spread rapidly westward toward the fall line. Indian clearings, known as "old fields," were grabbed up because they required no ground-clearing. Land fronting on deep water also was valued because ships could dock at bank-side, as at Jamestown. Even the largest oceangoing cargo ships in the seventeenth century drew no more than twelve feet of water.

For ease in handling, Virginians packed tobacco

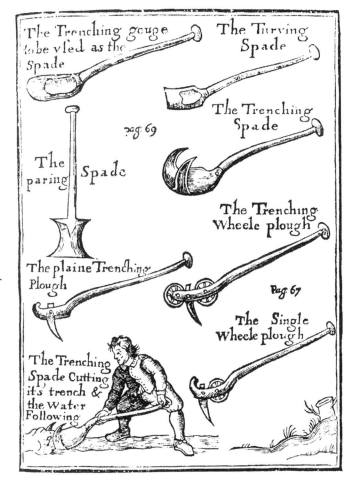

Plows and spades, such as those used in early Jamestown, were described for the planter in The English Improver Improved. *(From the Guildhall Library, London)*

in barrels called hogsheads. These were rolled by men or pulled by oxen or horses over "rolling roads" to plantation docks, there to be loaded aboard ship and stacked on end. To prevent the export of inferior leaf, the Burgesses in 1619 ordered that four viewers examine tobacco before shipment and that the worst be destroyed. By 1632 the Burgesses felt that additional inspection posts and warehouses were needed on the upper and lower James and along the York. Other warehouses were later built at other points, one of which survives today at Urbanna.

Rolfe's tobacco was known as Oronoco or Oronoko, for the Orinoco River basin in Venezuela, from which it came. Other early varieties were Trinidado, named for the West Indies island off the Venezuelan coast; and Varinas, which took its name from a South American town. The most desirable variety of all was Sweet-Scented, and especially that grown on Edward Digges' plantation, Chiskiack, now within the boundaries of the Naval Weapons Station at Yorktown. Digges' "York River" label brought a higher price than any other Virginia product. Its quality was attributed to the richness of the riverbank soil, for tobacco was a heavy feeder. England took all of Virginia's Sweet-Scented output, while sharing the Oronoco with Continental buyers.

Ignorant of soil chemistry, the early settlers repeated tobacco plantings in the same field each year until the soil was exhausted. This constant need for new fields hastened the spread of settlement upland along the tidal peninsulas in the seventeenth century to the fall line of the James, the York, the Rappahannock, and the Potomac rivers. Tobacco also made heavy demands on the grower. It required constant care from March, when the tiny seeds—ten thousand to a spoonful—were sifted into an

Tobacco hogsheads sit on a Virginia dock later in the seventeenth century awaiting shipment to England. (From an Elmo James drawing for Pierce Middleton, Tobacco Coast *[1953])*

outdoor seedbed, until late fall, when the cured leaf was placed in hogsheads to await shipment.

In May the seed germinated, and in June rows of plants were set in hillocks in cleared fields. One hard-working man could cultivate about 10,000 plants, occupying three or four acres. If the weather smiled, the plants were large enough by July to be topped, to limit each plant to no more than a dozen large leaves. Then the farmer must remove the "suckers" or offshoots from the main stem, and cut off the "lugs," or coarse bottom leaves. Full growth was reached by September. The plants then were cut down and allowed to wilt before being dried.

The first planters let tobacco cure in the sun, but they soon improved the process by tying stalks in "hands" and suspending them from rafters in curing houses, or barns. Sweet-Scented tobacco dried in three weeks, while the heavier Oronoco took six. The grower then waited until a rainy day when the dried leaf was pliable and piled the hands beneath a cloth cover to let it "sweat" by absorbing moisture. Sometimes the grower performed the further step of removing the stem from each leaf. In late fall the leaves were layered into a hogshead, compressed under force, and the barrel sealed, weighed, and marked with the owner's initials and insignia. Since handling and shipping costs were computed by hogshead, planters packed them tightly. If a dock was nearby, the hogsheads were rolled there. If not, they were floated by flatboat or sloop to the nearest dock or, after 1619, to the public warehouse for inspection and shipment.

In Virginia tobacco also was money. British currency controls limited the circulation of sterling outside the British Isles and inflicted untold hardships on colonial commerce. The colony's domestic trade as a result had to depend instead on tobacco notes, for Virginia was not permitted to issue a currency of her own. These tobacco notes transferred ownership of hogsheads from one man to another. Even the salaries of clergymen in seventeenth-century Virginia were specified in tobacco; a Sweet-Scented parish was preferred by a cleric to an Oronoco parish because it paid more. ❧

Planters and Pioneers: Life in Colonial Virginia, Hastings House Publishers, New York, 1968

CHAPTER 17

America's First Legislature

The scene at Jamestown that summer day in 1619 was one of earnest simplicity. Into the wooden church strode Governor Sir George Yeardley, handsomely dressed in silk doublet and breeches. Behind him came the six members of Virginia's Council, wearing hats and carrying swords.

While Yeardley took his seat in the Governor's pew near the pulpit, his councilors flanked him. Behind them, on rough-hewn benches, sat 22 tobacco farmers who had been elected as burgesses from the eleven "principal plantations," or settlements, in the 12-year-old colony.

Thus was representative government born in the New World: for this was the beginning of the Virginia General Assembly, the seed of Anglo-Saxon self-government which was ultimately to grow into the United States of America.

Though its legislative powers were few, the Assembly represented a victory for Parliamentary forces, which were slowly rising in England against Stuart absolutism. Behind it lay the scheming and battling of Sir Edwin Sandys, who had replaced Sir Thomas Smythe a year earlier, as head of the Virginia Company of London. So strong had been King James' aversion to Sandys' progressive "Country Party" that he had urged

This painting by an unidentified artist portrays the first meeting of the General Assembly in Virginia. (From the Richmond Times-Dispatch*)*

Company stockholders to "choose the Devil if you will, but not Sir Edwin Sandys." In spite of—or because of—this, Sandys had won.

Sandys was Virginia's champion in England, and it was he who sent Yeardley and legislative government to Virginia. Arriving at Jamestown early in 1619, armed with Sandys' Great Charter, Yeardley wasted no time persuading the Council that the infant colony (no more than 1,900 people) should be "reduced into four cities or burroughs, namely the chief city called James Town, Charles City, Henrico, and the Burrough of Kiccowtan."

Those first General Assembly meetings were held in the church at James Fort built about 1617. (From Jamestown Church at Historic Jamestown, Virginia*)*

This done, Yeardley had called for election by each James River and Eastern Shore settlement of two burgesses to meet with the governor and his Council at Jamestown, beginning July 30, "to establish equal and uniform government over all Virginia."

Like John Smith and other colonial governors, Yeardley had come up through the army's ranks. After a military career in the Low Countries, he had served Virginia for a year in 1616–17 as deputy governor under Lord de la Warr before returning to England. During his two years there he was chosen by Sandys and the Virginia Company to return to the colony as governor.

To strengthen his hand, King James I knighted him. In London, courtier John Chamberlain wrote to a friend on November 28, 1618: "Here be two or three ships redy for Virginia, and one Captain Yardley a meane [poor] fellow by way of provision goes as governor, and to grace him the more the King knighted him this weeke at Newmarket; which hath set him up so high that he flaunts yt up and downe the streets in extraordinaire braverie, with fowrteen or fifteen fayre liveries [uniformed servants] after him."

Sailing with Yeardley was his wife, Lady Temperance Flowerdieu, and her cousin, whom Yeardley had taken under his wing, 47-year-old John Pory. Chosen by Yeardley as secretary of his six-man Council, the accomplished Pory also served the first assembly in the important role of Speaker—the spokesman for the burgesses in their dealings with royal authority. In these two roles he both presided over the assembly and kept a daily written account, which he sent back to England.

From this admirable account, which Pory styled, "The Proceedings of the first assembly of Virginia—July 1619," we have authentic records of America's first legislature. This document is preserved today in England's Public Record Office in London.

Of those who made up the 1619 assembly, Pory was easily the best educated. Born of a well-connected family in Norfolk County, England, he was named for a great uncle who had been master of Corpus Christi College at Cambridge. At 16 he had entered Caius College at Cambridge, where he was graduated and became an instructor in Greek.

Pory's interest in Virginia no doubt grew out of his assistance to Richard Hakluyt, the geographer, in writing his epic, *The Principal Navigations, Voyages, Traffics, and Discoveries of the English Nation*, published in 1598–1600. Pory also had translated several important geographical works into English.

In 1605 Pory had been elected to Parliament, serving for six years during a period of rising tension between the autocratic James I and the increasingly outspoken Parliament. When James tried to stifle debate, the Commons asserted an "ancient general and undoubted right of Parliament to debate fully all matters which do properly concern the subject." Following his parliamentary years, he embarked on travels and correspondence throughout Europe.

Though Pory was a tippler ("Master Poorie must have both meal and monie, for drincke he will find out for himself," wrote a contemporary), Yeardley recommended him in October 1618, for a three-year term as secretary of the Virginia colony. Thus he came to Jamestown as the new governor's chief aide.

Immediately upon arrival, Governor Yeardley let it be known that the period of martial law established by Sir Thomas Dale in 1614 was ended. He informed Virginians by proclamation "that those cruell lawes, by which we had so long been governed, were now abrogated, and that we were to be governed by those free lawes, which his Majesties subjects live under in Englande." English common law was now in effect.

Under the terms of Sandys' Great Charter, the Virginia Company hoped to attract more families as permanent settlers in Virginia. A new effort was made to create towns, to sow crops other than tobacco, to open schools, and to build houses and inns.

Excitement was high-pitched in the lonely little settlements along the James as "titheables," or heads of household, chose their burgesses to go to Jamestown for the first assembly. Few of the names mean much today, for several were killed in the uprising of 1622 and most others died young.

The Council, whose members had been appointed for life by the Virginia Company, had one well-known member besides John Pory. He was John Rolfe, who had been married to Pocahontas until her death in England in 1617. The other members were Captain Francis West, Captain Nathaniel

The first legislative assembly in Virginia met at Jamestown in 1619. (From a Jack Glifton painting hanging in the Virginia Capitol, courtesy of the Library of Virginia)

Power, William Wickham, and Samuel Maycock.

The Virginia assembly followed many practices of England's Parliament, no doubt influenced by the experience of Pory. Each man vowed his loyalty to the crown in the Oath of Supremacy, which remained in effect throughout colonial times. In addition, the Assembly followed Parliament's practice since 1586 of determining the eligibility of its members. After a hearing, they refused to permit Davis and Stacy to represent Martin's Brandon (later Brandon Plantation in Prince George County) because it had been exempted from the laws of the colony in its initial grant.

(*Editor's note:* Following this tradition, the Virginia General Assembly and the United States Congress continue to this day to assert their right to pass on the validity of their members' election.)

It is clear from the record of the session that Pory was its dominant figure. His years in Parliament had familiarized him with legislative practices, and his acquaintance with Sandys and Yeardley gave him status, despite the fact that he had been at Jamestown only since April 19, or less than three months.

As the July sunlight streamed through the church windows, Pory proceeded to organize the assembly. First, he "delivered in briefe to the whole assembly the occasions of their meeting." Then he "read unto them the commission for establishing the Counsell of Estate and the general Assembly, wherein their duties were described to the life." Finally, he read Sandys' Great Charter that Yeardley had brought to Virginia as the new law.

Sir Thomas Dale was lieutenant governor of Virginia from 1614 to 1616 and left behind a legacy greatly changed by Governor Yeardley. (From the Virginia Museum of Fine Arts)

Clearly evident in Sandys' thinking was the Anglo-Saxon belief that society fares best under a republican government and a free economic system. Thus it builds upon the multiple ambitions, abilities, and interests of its members, within the framework of freedom. The Great Charter abolished martial law and Company ownership of land and tools, placed Virginia under the rule of law, and permitted colonists to elect representatives to share with the Virginia Company in making their laws.

It was a decision that would benefit British colonies in America until a stiffening of imperial policy under George III forced the colonies to revolt to obtain their rights.

After reading the Great Charter, Speaker Pory divided its provisions under four headings and appointed two committees of eight burgesses each to consider them. He directed each committee to determine which of the company's instructions "might conveniently putt on the habite of lawes."

But the burgesses did not depend on England alone for ideas. Pory asked each of them to decide also "what lawes might issue out of the private conceipte of any of the burgesses, or any other of the Colony." They also were to determine "what petitions were fitt to be sente home for England."

After the committees had left the church and deliberated, they returned the next day and reported. For one thing, they asked the Virginia Company to affirm that land grants by former governors to "antient Planters," be reconfirmed. Secondly, they urged the Company to rush settlers to build up the four would-be towns: James City, Charles City, Henrico, and Kecoughtan. Thirdly, they asked that the "ancient planters" who had come over at their own expense before Yeardley arrived in 1619 be assured of land grants for themselves, their sons, and daughters.

The burgesses also asked Sandys and the Virginia Company to send over workmen to build a proposed university at Henrico and the optimistic Sandys continued to push this project until the Indian uprising in 1622 showed the proposal to be premature. Not until the College of William and Mary was chartered in 1693 was this objective realized.

The Burgesses sweltered uncomfortably in Virginia's heat, for the summer of 1619 was a hot one. On Sunday, August 1, two days after the Assembly had convened, Burgess Walter Shelley of Smith's Hundred died of heat prostration. However, the Assembly reconvened on Monday without delay so that the burgesses could return promptly to their tobacco growing.

Entering its closing days, the Assembly passed laws against injury to the Indians and "Against Idlenes, Gaming, durunkenes, & excesse in apparel…" The latter, reflecting the feudal concept that underlings should not "dress above their station," stipulated that offenders be assessed fines in church.

Settlers were directed to be careful of their contact with Indians. They were "neither utterly to reject" the natives "nor yet to drawe them to come in" to their settlements. But it was recognized that the Indians could be useful "in killing of Deere, fishing, beating of Corne, and other workes," provided that "good guarde in the night be kept upon them."

The Assembly also directed each settlement to begin educating young Indians to prepare them for the university planned at Henrico. This again was part of the long-held hope that promising young Indians could be Christianized and sent as missionaries among the tribesmen.

In an effort to diversify the infant tobacco economy, every planter was directed to set out at least six mulberry trees for the next seven years to provide food for silkworms as raw material for a textile industry that never developed. Similarly, each man was directed to plant a hundred silk flax plants, ten grape vines, and such English flax and aniseed (for flavoring and medicine) as they had seed for. The search for saleable exports obviously began early in colonial America.

Having considered first the proposed laws sent from England and then those recommended by the governor in Virginia, the Assembly met August 3 and opened itself to individual proposals, "such as might proceed out of every mans private conceipts." In effect, it became a court of law, hearing accusations against individuals. And it wasted no time. One defendant, Thomas Garnett, was ordered to "stand fower dayes with his eares nailed to the Pillary…and every of those fower dayes should be publiquely whipped." Such was justice in colonial Virginia!

When the assembly met for the sixth day, on Wednesday, August 4, the heat at Jamestown continued to be overwhelming, and Governor Yeardley became ill. Sir Edwin Sandys' proposed laws had been enacted, along with others. According, the Assembly decided to end its deliberations that day.

Pory briskly noted all this in his Proceedings: "So in the morning the Speaker [as he was required by the Assembly] redd over all the lawes and orders that had formerly passed the house...to see whether there were any things to be amended."

Then, hurrying to finish before the hot August sun set across the James River shoreline, the Assembly received and passed 18 more proposals originated by members. These reflect the rough life they led in their little clearings on the James. These laws, the most revealing of the first Assembly's action, forbade the sale of English guns or dogs to the Indians, cautiously limited each settler's travels to 20 miles from home, forbade visits to Indian towns without authorization, prohibited the killing of cattle and the theft of boats or canoes, and prescribed duties of ministers and churchwardens.

Though Virginia was never as austere as the Massachusetts colony was to be, its Assembly enjoined against "Incontinency or of the commission of any other enormous sinnes." Offenders were to be tried by churchwardens. If they did not repent, they would be excommunicated from the church and their possessions seized.

Having penned 26 pages of the Proceedings, Pory wrote: "Here ende the lawes." But the Assembly was not yet adjourned. Lined up on their crude benches inside the church, its members still had to hear last-minute charges that Captain Henry Spelman, an Indian interpreter, had "alienated the minde" of Opechancanough, the chief who inherited Powhatan's kingdom. Spelman was tried and duly punished.

By this time, the sweltering Assemblymen were ready to quit. After agreeing to tax every male Virginian over 16 a pound of tobacco to compensate Pory and the "Clerke and Sergeant officers" of the Assembly, they rushed to go home. Commanding Speaker Pory to apologize to the Virginia Company of London for their sudden decision, they adjourned with instructions to Pory to send an account of their acts back to England.

"This they wholly committed to the fidelity of their speaker," he wrote, "who therein (his Conscience telles him) hath done the parte of an honest man."

Obviously, Pory was displeased with the Assembly's abrupt end, but members were sickening in the heat. Mounting their horses or their small riverboats—"pirogues" they later called them—the legislators hurried back to their homes before nightfall. Jamestown was not a healthy spot in the sultry summer.

Brief as the session had been, it made history. The next year, Bermuda's settlers held their first assembly. Then, one by one, England's other colonies followed. By 1650 the spirit and machinery of Anglo-Saxon lawmaking had been widely spread through the New World. Ultimately, it was to add to the ferment for American independence.

This National Park Service model of the meeting of the first legislature shows John Pory (seated center), who presided over the assembly and kept a daily written account. (From the Newport News **Daily Press***)*

And what of the chief contributors to Virginia's first assembly, Sir Edwin Sandys, Sir George Yeardley, and Master John Pory?

Sandys lived to see Virginia taken from the Virginia Company in 1624 and declared England's first royal colony. This action must have been a great disappointment to that tough, independent spirit.

Yeardley, after returning to England in 1621, came back to Jamestown for a second term as governor in 1626. There he died on November 12, 1627. What is believed to be his tombstone—a slate stone once inlaid with the brass figure of a knight—now rests in the reconstructed Jamestown Church.

As for Pory, he continued to perform services for Virginia. He was lauded by the Assembly in 1619 as the man "who not only first formed the same Assembly and to their great ease and expedition reduced all matters to be treated of into a ready method, but also ... wrote or dictated all orders and other expedients and is yet to write several bookes for all the General Incorporations and plantation both of the great Charter, and of all the lawes."

Pory remained a rolling stone. For his service to Yeardley and the Assembly, he was granted the use of a 500-acre plantation in Northampton County on the Eastern

Shore, but this passed to his successor when Pory returned to England in 1622. In his three years in Virginia, however, he had successfully worked to realize Sandys' ambitions for the colony. He also sent useful advice back to the London Company, encouraged establishment of the first American iron works at Falling Creek, and pointed out a more efficient method of producing salt.

After a year in England, Pory was appointed to a royal commission created by King James I to inquire into affairs in unprofitable Virginia. He and fellow commissioner John Harvey came back to Virginia in 1624 and stayed several months. When they returned to England, however, they found the Crown had already taken control of Virginia, now no longer a private venture, but England's first royal colony.

The scholarly bachelor spent the end of his life in England, writing newsletters and corresponding with geographers. He died in Lincolnshire in 1635, leaving three acres of land to his parish church, Sutton St. Edmund. Twice a year since then, the rector has preached the Pory "Commemoration Sermons" required by his gift.

Sir Edwin Sandys was chosen head of the Virginia Company of London in 1618 and was instrumental in George Yeardley being appointed governor. Sandys encouraged Yeardley to pursue an elected assembly. (From Parke Rouse Jr., Virginia—The English Heritage in America*)*

As to the other members of the Assembly, several were killed by Opechancanough's tribesmen in their uprising in 1622. Only a few were to be well-remembered: Francis West became governor from 1627–29, Captain Thomas Graves became commander of the plantation of Accomack, and John Rolfe made tobacco Virginia's salvation.

As for the Assembly itself, it slowly gained strength despite the disdain of arrogant Stuart kings. Within 150 years, its burgesses (by then removed to Williamsburg) dared to meet in rump session and defy British might. The spirit of independence led Patrick Henry to cry out, "Give me liberty or give me death." The Revolution had begun.

The Assembly envisioned by Sandys had learned its lessons well. Colonial Americans increasingly came to expect the rights that "freeborn Englishmen" had so dearly won in the

The Reconstructed church at Jamestown Festival Park was the site of this re-enactment in the mid-twentieth century of the first legislative assembly in America. (From the collection of the Jamestown-Yorktown Foundation)

years since the barons of Runnymede had forced King John to sign the Magna Carta. In a very real sense, George Mason's Bill of Rights and Thomas Jefferson's Declaration of Independence grew out of that first assembly in the simple wooden church at Jamestown. ❦

The Iron Worker, Winter, 1971, Lynchburg Foundry Company

CHAPTER 18

The Slaves

A Dutch frigate docked at Point Comfort (in today's Hampton) in 1619 and traded 20 black slaves to Virginia settlers in return for goods. Thus African servitude began in Virginia, spreading through the colonies until arrested 244 years later by the Emancipation Proclamation.

The first Virginian blacks had been captured on the Guinea coast of Africa, where warring tribes for centuries had sold captives into slavery. While a novelty in English America, nearly 900,000 enslaved Africans already had been brought to Spanish and Portuguese colonies and mines in South America, crowded in dark squalor aboard slave ships. Nearly 3,000,000 were brought to the Americas in the seventeenth century, the influx rising to 7,000,000 in the eighteenth century.

Slave traders had visited Africa since the Middle Ages, and bartered mirrors, beads, cloth, and rum for black people. From West Africa, in the Sudan, they took tall blue-black Wolof and Hausa tribesmen. From the equatorial forest in the south they led away thousands of other "bush" blacks, who were shorter of stature and lighter of color than the Sudanese. To obtain European goods, African chieftains sold even their kinsmen to Europeans. Villages were burned and whole communities were seized and herded into corrals to await sale and shipment to the New World or Europe.

In 1619 English sea captain John Hawkins entered the slave trade in competition with the Dutch and Portuguese. Before the century had ended, these three maritime powers operated nearly forty factories, as they were called, on Africa's coast to buy and sell slaves. In 1663, after the Navigation Acts had restricted colonists' trade to the mother country, England gave to its Royal African Company a monopoly on slave trade to the English colonies. The booming business was opened up to all English subjects 35 years later.

Traders bought only able-bodied blacks, leaving the old and sick to die in factory corrals. Once aboard ship, the captives were chained to the deck to prevent escape or insurrection. Equatorial heat and shipboard diseases killed many, about 15 percent dying in transit. One vessel reaching Virginia in 1702 lost 100 of its original 330 slaves at sea.

The first blacks in Virginia were treated as indentured servants, probably just a

The first blacks arrived from Africa in Virginia in 1619, brought by a Dutch trading vessel.
(From a Sidney E. King painting, courtesy of the Colonial Williamsburg Foundation)

legalized fiction because few found any end to their servitude. In the first Jamestown census in 1625, records account for 10 slaves. There were only about 300 in the colony in 1649, but the Virginia economy was booming and the need for agriculture workers increased. Thus, slavery—the cheapest form of labor—increased. By 1671 slaves accounted for five percent (or 2,000) of Virginia's population of roughly 40,000 persons, and the slavery numbers increased to 24 percent by 1715.

If there were truly any indentured black servants in Virginia, they were all but wiped out by growing numbers of laws. In fact, free blacks were banished from Virginia by legislation in 1661. The next year, a law stated simply that Africans were in service for life.

A rise in tobacco prices after 1670 spurred slavery's growth in Virginia for the next hundred years. William Byrd II complained in 1736 that Virginia "will some time or another be confirmed by the name of New Guinea," but importation of slaves was not forbidden in Virginia until 1774. By the time of the American Revolution, blacks accounted for nearly half of Virginia's population.

Slaves became a major source of England's riches. Bought at African factories for £4 to £20 apiece, they were sold in the colonies at prices ranging from £16 in the seventeenth century to £40 by 1750 and £100 by 1775. Top prices were paid for carpenters and craftsmen. Slaves sold faster in the growing season, when planters needed them to work the fields. In Virginia's barter economy, merchants or planters with good credit bought many on consignment.

Shippers in Bristol and later in Liverpool sent more than 100,000 Guineamen and women each year from slave factories on Africa's Gold Coast to the West Indies and North America. The Virginia colony tried to halt the flood, but the Crown forbade it. England's Board of Trade also annulled import taxes, which Virginia's General Assembly had imposed in an effort to control the flow. The Crown's encouragement of the trade confirmed Virginia's opposition to British trade policy; in the recital of Britain's offenses, which he included in his first draft of the Declaration of Independence, Thomas Jefferson cited Britain's slave trade.

The colonists themselves finally entered the profitable trade. After the Royal African Company's monopoly was ended in 1678, Virginia vessels brought slaves from the West Indies. New England merchants began slave trading on a larger scale after

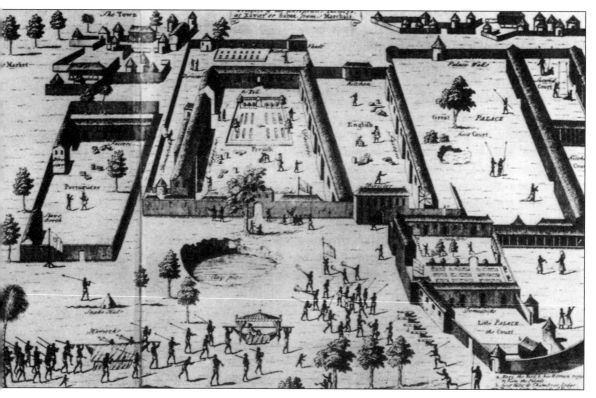

At slave markets or factories on the African coast, tribal chiefs sold their war captives to European traders. They were kept in corrals until sold as slaves. (From Virginia: History, Government and Geography *[1957])*

1737, building ships with hundreds of slave cells. Returning from Africa with a full cargo, the merchants traded them in the West Indies or southern colonies for products needed in New England. Boston and Newport were centers of this trade, which enriched many shipmasters and merchants.

Virginians at first feared the newcomers and their "black magic." Eventually Virginia law prohibited blacks from holding any "office, civil, ecclesiastic, or military, or any place of public trust or power." The colony's policy from 1607 had opposed settlers' cohabitation with Indians, and similar laws eventually were passed applying to relationships between blacks and whites. ⚜

Slaves are depicted packing tobacco for shipment to England in this detail from a late seventeenth-century engraving. (From Marshall W. Fishwick, Jamestown: First English Colony *[1965])*

Planters and Pioneers—Life in Colonial Virginia, Hastings House Publishers, New York, 1968

CHAPTER 19 ✤

The Indian Attack of 1622

From the earliest days of settlement, despite efforts of the English colonists to coexist peaceably with the native tribes, there was little peace. Both sides took hostages periodically as insurance against an attack, and cruelty often saw no bounds.

John Rolfe's marriage to Pocahontas in 1614 brought the first element of peace to the region until her chief-father Powhatan died in 1618 and was succeeded by his younger brother, Opechancanough. For the next several years, coexistence became more and more difficult because Opechancanough disliked the settlers intensely and did everything he could to foment problems.

Benson J. Lossing in his book *Our Country* explained that Opechancanough, with the ability to command thousands of warriors to do his bidding, "feigned friendship" for the colonists, and "deceived them with Satanic smiles. He believed that the English intended to seize the lands of his empire and exterminate his race, and his patriotism impelled him to strike a blow for his country and countrymen."

Finally he ordered the attack. On Good Friday morn-

This engraving depicts a 1608 encounter between Captain John Smith and Opechancanough, Chief Powhatan's brother, who led the Indian attack against the settlers in March 1622. (From The Generall Historie of Virginia, New-England and the Summer Isles, *London [1624], courtesy of the editor.)*

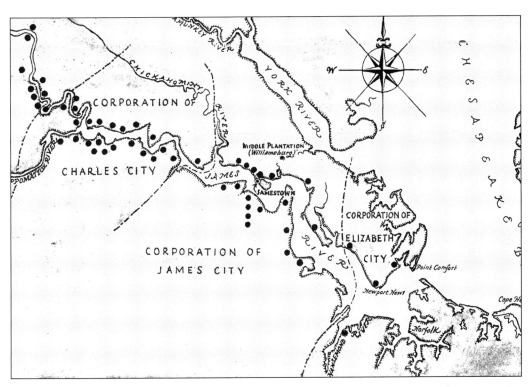

In this map of 1622 Virginia, the dotted lines show the boundaries between counties [corporations] while the dots represent the individual settlements at the time of the Indian attacks. (From Marshall W. Fishwick, Jamestown, First English Colony *[1957]*

ing, March 22, 1622, the Algonquins fell upon the scattered English farms and settlements, killing 347 of the 1,250 settlers along the banks of the James River.

Writing in her book *Virginia's First Century*, Mary Newton Stanard said the attack "was as thoroughly managed as if the natives had had telegraphic facilities and the secret was so completely kept that no suspicion entered the heart of a colonist. The Indians kept up their appearance of friendship till the moment when they had been ordered to strike."

Samuel Purchas, an English clergyman and compiler of travel literature, wrote, "Some of them were even sitting down at breakfast with our people at their tables" when the eight o'clock attack occurred. The Indians "rose up as one man and each began murdering the pale face friends who happened to be closest to him," Stanard wrote. "Neither aged man and women nor young children were spared. Each uplifted tomahawk fell upon the victim nearest the hand that wielded it so suddenly that few or none discerned the weapon that brought them to destruction."

Continuing, Stanard recounted, "Purchas, quoting letters from Virginia, says that converted Indians saved the lives of some of the colonists. The Indians lived in small, widely scattered settlements, yet all received notice when to strike and directions as to what places they were to attack. By letters and from those who returned to England it was 'certified that (besides Master George Thorpe) Master John

Berkeley, Captain Nathaniel Power and his wife, and Captain Maycocke—all gentle-men of birth, virtue, and industry, and of the Council there, suffered under this their cruelty and treason.' "

Robert Beverley's account of the attack says the Indians "to color their design the better, brought presents of deer, turkey, fish, and fruits to the English the evening before. The very morning of the attack they came freely and unarmed among them, eating with them and behaving themselves with the same freedom and friendship as formerly till the very minute they were to put their plot in execution." When they attacked, the Indians used their hatchets or tomahawks and even hoes and axes used by their English "friends."

At Henrico, the most westward English enclave, the Indians virtually wiped out the settlement. So bad was the situation that it took many years for Henrico to be reestablished, and the college planned for the area never materialized.

At Jamestown an Indian, Chanco, who had befriended the settlement, warned the colonists, and while they suffered an attack, the settlement survived. Apparently, several nights before the attack, Opechancanough came to him to per-suade him to murder the family with whom he lived at the same time the other attacks would take place up and down the river. Chanco, however, could not

In this European view of the Indian uprising of 1622, the Indians plunder an outlying settlement, while a war party in canoes approaches Jamestown [background]. (From Theodor de Bry, America, **Part XIII** *[1628])*

There had been many Indian attacks on the settlers, such as the one pictured above, but none as devastating as the 1622 events that hit nearly every settlement along the James River. (From a postal card published by the Jamestown Amusement & Vending Co., Norfolk, for the 1907 Jamestown Exposition, courtesy of the editor)

turn upon his friends and told of the pending assault.

Stanard wrote that by late afternoon on March 22 "Governor Yeardley went in his ship up the river to Flowerdieu Hundred to give aid to those who might be wounded." A list of those killed included 73 at Martin's Hundred, where Wolstenholm Towne was located and the site of present-day Carter's Grove Plantation. Wolstenholm was a primitive palisaded settlement in what would become James City County, and the Indians not only attacked the stockade, but also the surrounding houses and huts, killing nearly everyone in sight.

The settlement was accidentally discovered in 1970 by an archaeological team under the direction of Ivor Noël Hume from Colonial Williamsburg, while seeking the remains of early Carter's Grove outbuildings. What they found, in addition to the palisades and related buildings, were the long-lost skeletons of men, women, and children who died cruelly in what the English would call "the massacre."

Since discovery, Wolstenholm Towne has become internationally known and was the subject of a major article by Noël Hume in the National Geographic magazine and of a book by him, *Martin's Hundred*, published in 1982 by Alfred Knopf.

Noël Hume and his archaeological team stumbled across skeletons of Wolstenholm residents lying apparently as they fell when attacked by the Indians long ago. In several cases tomahawks apparently had pierced their skulls, and their scalps had been removed.

After 1622 the English treated the Indians with greater severity, waging war

A conjectural sketch of the Indian attack at the iron furnace at Falling Creek, up river from Jamestown. (From A Pictorial Booklet on Early Jamestown Commodities and Industries, The Virginia 350th Anniversary Celebration Corporation.)

against them until 1636. A second Indian uprising in 1644 permanently estranged the two peoples. Opechancanough was behind that attack, too, and was later captured and taken to Jamestown, where a soldier killed him. The dwindling tribes were pushed farther and farther westward, and a treaty confined some of them on two reservations—on the Mattaponi and Pamunkey rivers. The reservations survive today and were the first established by any government in the English colonies. By 1665 Powhatan's people in Tidewater were dependent on the English, and their independent lifestyle had been lost. 🏺

The Iron Worker, Winter, 1963–1964, Lynchburg Foundry Co., and
The James—Where a Nation Began, The Dietz Press, Richmond, 1990

CHAPTER 20 ✿

Roads and Waterways of Early Virginia

No aspect of life in Virginia has changed as much in the 400 years since Jamestown as the way Americans travel. Whereas John Rolfe could cover 20 miles a day on foot or 100 miles by sailboat, today's motorist can easily log 500 miles or more. The rapid movement of people and of video images in the past 50 years along has shrunk the globe and made the moon a near neighbor.

In such an age, it is hard to realize that Americans for 250 years moved at the leisurely pace of the horse, the ox, and the riverboat. Travel then was so arduous that many people never ventured outside their home communities or counties. Yet the writings of pioneers like Captain John Smith, William Byrd II, and later Daniel Boone reflect the frequent pleasures of travel as well as its rigors. Discomfort abounded but, like Chaucer's pilgrims en route to Canterbury, the adventurers found camaraderie and often inspiration along the way.

Before the age of the automobile, travel in Virginia could be divided into seven roughly overlapping phases: the age of Indian trails; the first settlers' initial reliance on water travel; the growth of a coastal "King's Highway" linking Virginia with Maryland and North Carolina; the development of a western Virginia wagon road; the penetration of the Tennessee and Kentucky territories by the Wilderness Trail; the creation of the James River and Potomac River canal systems; and the revolutionary onslaught of the railroads. Herein the

Boats hauled people and products like these Virginia tobacco boats that coped with the shallow creeks and streams taking golden "money" to ports. (From Alfred Percy, Piedmont Apocalypse, *Madison Heights, Virginia [1949])*

discussion will focus on the first two phases.

Indians had blazed the trails that crisscrossed Virginia long before the first settlers arrived in 1607. Some of these prehistoric trails followed the earlier paths of buffalo herds, while others had been cut by migrating Indians to take advantage of streambeds, mountain passes, salt licks, fresh springs, and other natural features. Virginia's settlers in colonial times took over these routes as footpaths, spreading steadily outward from the first beachhead at Jamestown.

One major Indian route began at the point later called Bermuda Hundred, on the south shore of the James River. From that point, the trail led south through what later became Petersburg and southwest to the present Clarksville on the Roanoke River. It was called the Occonneechee Path because it led to the fortified inland town of the Occonneechee Indians, who dominated the Indian trade of the upper south until the rebel Nathaniel Bacon destroyed their town in 1676. From the Roanoke River, the path led southward to the lands of the Catawbas and the Cherokees in the Carolinas.

Another prehistoric path led from the south shore of the James in present-day Richmond, westward to the towns of the Saponi and Totero Indians, near the present cities of Lynchburg and Roanoke. Some earlier settlers acquired wealth through the trade of baubles for the Indians' furs; laden pack-trains brought thousands of beaver, marten, and other furs to the eastern settlements, from which they were shipped to England.

The most important Indian travel in Virginia, however, was the path used by Iroquois raiders from upstate New York on their periodic raids southward against the smaller tribes of inland Virginia and the Carolinas. Called the Appalachian Warriors' Path or the Iroquois Traders' Path, this route followed the valley through western Virginia from the Potomac River on the north to the western tip of Tennessee, the region of the Watauga, Holston and Nolichucky rivers.

The word "path" was commonly used then to mean a narrow forest clearing,

At the outset, few wagons, like this seventeenth century English vehicle, were used in Virginia because of a lack of roads. (From David Loggan, Oxonia Illustrata *[1675])*

Carts were easier to use than wagons because they could be pulled over the worst terrain. (From David Loggan, Oxonia Illustrata *[1675])*

wide enough only for a man or an animal. A cart path was one traversed by a two-wheeled vehicle pulled by horse or ox. A road or wagon road was wide enough for four-wheeled vehicles, including the heavy-wheeled covered carryall that came to be known as the Conestoga or covered wagon. Other two-wheeled vehicles besides carts were called chairs, chaises and, later, jumpers.

But Virginia's rivers were the real highways for the earliest English settlers as used by John Smith in his early explorations around the Chesapeake Bay in 1607 and 1608s. So extensive were the creeks and rivers of the Chesapeake basin that the early Virginia houses were built facing river docks. Sailboats of various types—pinnaces, sloops, scows, pinks, and schooners among them—were used in open water; hollowed logs called pirogues, dugouts, log canoes, rowboats called shallops, row galleys, and bateaux were all common. To serve as ferries, flat scows and wide barges were used.

To load the Dutch, Portuguese, and English ships that in the early seventeenth-century trade in Virginia, hogsheads of tobacco were pushed over "rolling roads" to docks on the James and later the York, Rappahannock, or Potomac. The importance of deepwater docks was shown in the settlers' selection of Jamestown as their capital for Virginia's first 92 years.

The cutting of roads was left for the first several decades to landowners. Then, in 1632, a move was made towards community thoroughfares. In that year, the Assembly at Jamestown ordered that "highways shall be laid out in such convenient places as are requisite according as the Governor and Council or the Commissions for the monthly courts shall appoint, or according as the parishioners of every parish shall agree." A few years later, the assembly ordered "all general ways from county to county and all churchways [are] to be laid out and cleared yearly." ✥

The Iron Worker, Spring, 1973, Lynchburg Foundry Company

CHAPTER 21

The Colony's Outdoor Life

Virginia was part of the frontier of European civilization through colonial times. The three-cornered palisade at Jamestown in 1607 was not far different in design from the blockhouse that Daniel Boone built nearly two centuries later, in 1774, to ward off the Indians at Bonesborough. Most of those early Virginians grew up in an untamed land, fearing the insurrection of Indians and later slaves. Only the fit and fortunate lived out a normal life span.

The bantam, cocky John Smith was the classic Virginia outdoorsman. Scorning the safety of James Fort, he explored lowland Virginia for two years to map it and trade with its Indians before turning to England. He was the first of many explorers and fighters to gain fame in Virginia: the Indian traders Abraham Wood and William Byrd I in the first century, and later Alexander Spotswood, George Washington, Dr. Thomas Walker, Daniel Boone, and many others in the second century.

Like many frontier societies, Virginia valued bravery as the highest virtue. It was true at Jamestown beginning with the day of arrival. The settlers brought weapons with them and a portion of them were always on duty for militia work.

From the outset hunting in Virginia was difficult because of the heavy matchlock muskets used by the colonists. Notice the bandoleer over the shoulder containing charges of powder and the spike used to support the gun barrel when firing. (From a British Library woodcut)

Guns brought from England to Jamestown were matchlock muskets that were so heavy, the barrel had to be rested on a support to be fired with any accuracy. These primitive weapons were loaded with loose powder from small vials that the musketeer suspended from a bandoleer, worn from shoulder to waist, and fired by match. Such unwieldy weapons were slow to fire, and their loose powder was dangerous, as Captain Smith learned when the powder pouch on his belt prematurely exploded in 1609.

The wheelock, whose powder was ignited by sparks from a built-in flint, succeeded the matchlock. Later in the early eighteenth century came the improved flintlock small-bore rifle. Hunting was widely enjoyed. Great flights of wild ducks and geese passed over Virginia each year in their migratory journey. These and deer, wild turkey, partridge, sora, doves, and quail were considered proper for eating and sporting.

The most coveted quarry for early Nimrods were buffalo that were first described by Captain Samuel Argall in a voyage up the Potomac in 1613. The animals chiefly frequented the Valley of Virginia, where Indians hunted them endlessly.

The tidal waters of Virginia and the Chesapeake Bay abounded with food for Indians and settlers alike. Shad, herring, bass, black and red drum, carp, perch, crab, oyster, mussel, flounder, and dozens of other varieties of fish provided an immediate source of food for the settlers, who were helped, on occasions, by friendly Indians

Friendly Indians taught the early settlers how to fish and to cook in their new wilderness. (Engraved by Theodor de Bry in 1590 from Thomas Hariot's Admiranda Narratio fida tamen, de Commodis et Incolarum Ritibus Virginiae, *Frankfurt, [1590])*

These artifacts—fishhooks, fish-gigs, and lead net-weights —excavated at Jamestown are reminders of a day when fish and shellfish were a main food staple for the settlers. (From the National Park Service, Colonial National Historical Park)

who had mastered the art of fishing and enjoyed spearing fish in the hours of darkness.

Smith said of the Chesapeake region that "heaven and earth never agreed to frame a better place for man's habitation." Another early Jamestown settler, Gentleman George Percy, described the land around the Bar as "fair meadows and goodly tall trees with such fresh water...as I was almost ravished at the first sight there...We ate some of the oysters, which were very large and delicate in taste."

Fishing later proved a popular sport, both in the Chesapeake's estuaries and in freshwater ponds further inland, where anglers trolled for fish, using silk or horsehair lines. Indians of the Jamestown era fished for sturgeon with arrow-tipped spears, often using a long canoe hollowed by fire and stone hatchet.

As the settlements of early Virginia grew from shoreline to inland communities and towns, so did the outdoor life of the settlers expand. From sustenance activities— hunting and fishing for food—life moved to hunting and fishing for sport, such as fly fishing of the late seventeenth century and thoroughbred racing and riding to hounds in pursuit of a fox in the early eighteenth century. 🎐

Planters and Pioneers—Life in Colonial Virginia, Hastings House Publishers, New York, 1968

(Left) Indians fished for sturgeon with arrow-tipped spears. Jamestown Festival interpreter James Ware from the Rappahannock Tribe used a log canoe hollowed by fire and stone hatchet. (From the Jamestown-Yorktown Foundation, photo by Chiles T. Larson)

(Right) Tidewater Virginia was pierced by hundreds of streams in which fish abounded. (From Braun & Hogenberg, Civitatis Orbis Terrarum [1575])

CHAPTER 22

The Tradescants: Early Naturalists

After Virginia was settled, Englishmen immediately became curious about what grew there. A few daring English explorers and naturalists even crossed the ocean and brought back animals and plant specimens to the British Isles to be admired and identified.

One of the most appealing of the voyaging naturalists was John Tradescant, the Younger. (The name is pronounced *Tra-DES-cant*.) A royal gardener to England's Kings Charles I and II, he braved the Atlantic at least three times.

Now John Tradescant and his father—who also was a gardener to the king—have been honored by the formation of a Tradescant research group and an international horticultural museum at St. Mary's Church in Lambeth, in London. Plant and animal exhibits in this Tradescant Gardeners Museum include some plants that John Tradescant the Younger brought back.

Current interest in the little-known Tradescants began in 1964, when naturalist Mea Allen published in London the first study of their lives. Titled *The Tradescants: Their Plants, Gardens and Museum, 1570-1662*, it helped to explain how Europeans came to

John Tradescant the elder began a London museum that was later given to Oxford University as the Ashmolean Museum. (From the Ashmolean Museum via the Rouse Collection, Earl Gregg Swem Library, College of William and Mary)

know such New World oddities as the opossum, raccoon, and such plants as the climber Englishmen called the Virginia creeper.

It is believed by some that the younger Tradescant is responsible for the presence in England for nearly 400 years of "Powhatan's mantle," a deerhide hanging

decorated with small shells. (See Chapter 30.) It is one of many early Virginia items of Tradescant that ultimately came into the possession of antiquarian Elias Ashmole whose collection in 1683 became the Ashmolean Museum at Oxford University.

Because their lives spanned 92 eventful years of Virginian and English history, the Tradescants have become an important international cultural link. The Tradescants gained their odd name in medieval England, when they "treaded" or tanned skins, or hides.

The elder John was born in London in 1550 and developed gardens that still survive at Hatfield House, the seat near London of the Cecil family. To landscape the gardens, Tradescant journeyed over Europe and collected exotic species of plants and trees to bring to England.

The self-taught naturalist also collected stuffed animals, natural oddities, and other "rarities," as he called them, to

John Tradescant the younger made three or four voyages to Virginia to collect curiosities. (From the Ashmolean Museum via the Rouse Collection, Earl Gregg Swem Library, College of William and Mary)

exhibit at his house and garden in the South Lambeth part of London. Eventually he opened his house to the public as a "Closett of Rarities"—the first public museum in the British Isles.

The elder Tradescant was a friend of Captain John Smith of the Jamestown settlement. When Smith returned from his last North American expedition and died in England, he left Tradescant senior several books from his sea chest. It is thought that these inspired John Tradescant junior—born in 1608—to come to Virginia and see it for himself.

Little is known of the three trips young John made to Virginia, except the dates. However, Sir John Williamson, the keeper of King Charles II's library at Whitehall, wrote that "in 1637 John Tradescant was in the colony, to gather all rarities of flowers, plants, shells, etc."

After Tradescant senior died, the younger returned to Virginia twice—in 1642

Many Virginia plants and animals, unknown in England, were sent back by early settlers and visitors, such as John Tradescant the younger. (From the Colonial Williamsburg Foundation)

and again in 1654. In October of 1642 he was granted headrights for 650 acres of land on the north side of the Charles River, now the York. They were located on "Payanketank" or Piankitank Creek in what is now Gloucester County. The grant acknowledged that Tradescant had brought 13 new settlers to Virginia, for each of whom he received 50 acres.

Scholars believe the naturalist was encouraged to visit Virginia where Edward Digges, a planter who lived near the present Yorktown, was probably his host. Digges was the son of Sir Dudley Digges of Kent, England, with whom Tradescant senior had voyaged to Russia. Edward Digges was helpful in recording facts about New World animals and plants. His "sweet-scented" tobacco, which he developed in early Virginia and sent to England, brought the highest prices of any Virginia leaf.

Like a few other amateur naturalists of the time, the Tradescants sought to classify plants and animals scientifically. In this they anticipated the binomial method introduced by the Swedish botanist Karl Linnaeus in his *Systema Naturae* in 1735. Wrote their biographer, Mea Allen: "The Tradescants in their work, which was truly scientific, were far ahead of scientists in other fields, for those were still in their crude beginnings."

The Tradescant museum at "The Ark," in London's section called Lambeth because it surrounds Lambeth Palace, the traditional home of the Archbishop of

Canterbury, grew to contain many curiosities to attract visitors. One observer wrote of John junior, "Of flowers he has a good choice; and his Virginia and other birds in a great variety, with his glass hive, add much to the pleasure of his garden." An adventurer named Peter Munday, who had sailed for England's East Indian Company and was about to depart for China, wrote about his visit:

"I was invited by Mr. Thomas Barlow to view some rarities at John [Tradescant's], soe went with him and one friend more, there to spend the whole day in peruseings and that superficially, such as hee had gathered together... Moreover, a little garden with divers outlandish herbes and flowers, where of some that I had not seene elsewhere but in Indian, being supplied by Noblemen, Gentlemen, Sea Commanders, etts..."

One of the plants in the Tradescant garden was "Silke Grasse that groweth" in Virginia. We know it today as spiderwort, or flower-of-a-day. In England it came to be known as "Tradescant his Spiderwort" and was catalogued later by Linnaeus as *Tradescantia virginiana*. Botanist currently use it in experiments to determine factors in plant heredity.

Some of the exotic plants catalogued by the Tradescants in their Lambeth museum were Virginia cranesbill, persimmon, New England strawberry, Virginia creeper, Virginia yucca, Virginia nettle tree of hackberry, Virginia mulberry, Virginia arsmart, Tulip tree, Virginia evergreen thorn, Virginia crawfood, Virginia bladdernut, riverbank grape, and Virginia fox grape.

The Tradescant family tomb is located in the churchyard of St. Mary-at-Lambeth, now the Museum of Garden History. (From the Museum of Garden History, London)

Before he died, John Tradescant the Younger made a catalogue of his "rarities" in 1656, published as *Musaeum Tradescantianum*. Among his "Principall Benefactors," he lists many early patrons or explorers of Virginia including Sir Thomas Smythe, onetime head of the Virginia Company; Sir Dudley Digges; and 11 ship's captains. Some benefactors reflect the esteem the Tradescants enjoyed as men of science. These include King Charles I and his queen; George Villiers, duke of Buckingham; William Laud, Archbishop of Canterbury; two successive Earls of Salisbury; and Viscount Falkland, for whom the Falkland Islands were named.

The Tradescants' lives reveal that Englishmen were not only concerned to add wealth but also wanted to learn more about the brave new world of Virginia and the other British colonies abroad.

In London, visitors to the Museum of Garden History at Lambeth will encounter the tombstone in St. Mary's Churchyard of three generations of Tradescants—the last one the son of John junior, who died as a boy. The handsome seventeenth-century memorial bears these words:

> Know, stranger, ere thou pass, beneath this stone,
> Lye John Tradescant, grandsire, father, son,
> The last dy'd in his spring, the other two
> Liv'd till they had travell'd Orb and Natural through,
> As by their choice Collections may appear,
> Of what is rare, in land, in sea, in air:
> Whilst they (as Homer's *Iliad* in a nut)
> A world of wonders in one closet shut,
> These famous Antiquarians that had been
> Both Gardeners to the Rose and Lily Queen,
> Transplanted now themselves, sleep here;
>   And when
> Angels shall with their trumpets waken men,
> And fires shall purge the world, these three shall rise
> And Change this garden then for Paradise.

Like Charles Darwin and his voyage on the *Beagle* more than a century later, the Tradescants help us know our universe. Their "world of wonders" has become ours. 🕸

The James—Where A Nation Began, The Dietz Press, Richmond, 1990

Part II
Jamestown Vignettes

*Since 1957 reproductions of the three Jamestown ships—*Susan Constant, Godspeed *and* Discovery—*have been a major attraction at the Jamestown Festival Park, now called Jamestown Settlement. This photograph is from the mid-1960s. (From the Jamestown-Yorktown Foundation, courtesy of the* Richmond Times-Dispatch)

CHAPTER 23

1588 Book Advertises Virginia

The first book ever written about Virginia came from a London press in February 1588—a full 19 years before the settlement of Jamestown. The book, *A Brief and True Report of the New Found Land of Virginia*, helped persuade the English that the Chesapeake region of North America should be settled by Englishmen.

The rest, as they say, is history.

The book was written by Thomas Hariot, an English mathematician and tutor of Sir Walter Raleigh, who sent him to explore America in 1585 under the leadership of Sir Richard Grenville. Two years later, Raleigh sent out another expedition, which vanished in what is now North Carolina.

After Raleigh's "Lost Colony" disappeared, England had to wait until 1607 to settle Virginia at Jamestown.

The 1585 expedition made two significant contributions to Europe's knowledge of the New World. The first was Hariot's exciting "Report," which was published in London in 1588 and reprinted in Frankfurt in 1590, and which infected Europeans with a sort of New World fever. The second was the watercolor paintings of Indians, flora, and fauna made by John White, which provided an unsurpassed view of Virginia's Algonquin primitives. White's watercolors were first reproduced as line drawings in Theodore de Bry's reprinting of Hariot's "Report," turned out in Frankfurt in 1590 in Latin, French, German, and English.

Only six copies of Hariot's 1588 printing survive, each valued at more than

Thomas Hariot (or Harriot), the Oxford University mathematician and cartographer, compiled a large scientific catalogue of information on the geography and wildlife of Virginia. (From the President and Fellows of Trinity College, Oxford)

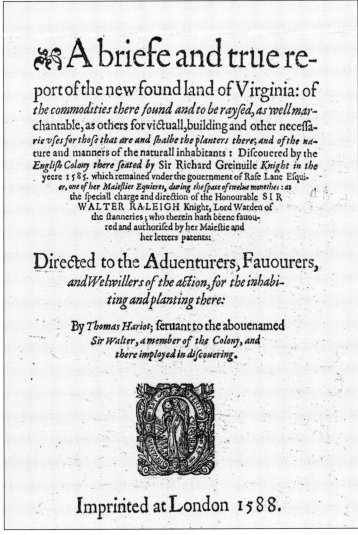

A briefe and true re-
port of the new found land of Virginia: of
the commodities there found and to be rayſed, as well mar-
chantable, as others for victuall, building and other neceſſa-
rie vſes for thoſe that are and ſhalbe the planters there; and of the na-
ture and manners of the naturall inhabitants : Diſcouered by the
Engliſh Colony there ſeated by Sir Richard Greinuile *Knight in the*
yeere 1585. which remained vnder the gouernment of Rafe Lane Eſqui-
er, one of her Maieſties Eſquiers, during theſpace of twelue monethes : at
the ſpeciall charge and direction of the Honourable S I R
WALTER RALEIGH Knight, Lord Warden of
the ſtanneries ; who therein hath béene fauou-
red and authoriſed by her Maieſtie and
her letters patents:

Directed to the Aduenturers, Fauourers,
and Welwillers of the action, for the inhabi-
ting and planting there:

By *Thomas Hariot*; ſeruant to the abouenamed
Sir Walter, a member of the Colony, and
there imployed in diſcouering.

Imprinted at London 1588.

The first book written about Virginia was published in 1588: A Brief and True Report of the New Found Land of Virginia. *(From the Rouse Collection in the Earl Gregg Swem Library, College of William and Mary)*

$500,000. They are at Oxford and Loydon universities, the British Museum, the Huntington Museum, the University of Michigan, and the New York Public Library. The College of William and Mary's library owns a rare edition, dating from 1608.

History records little about Hariot, but one can tell from his little book that he was an acute observer. So far as is known, he was the first European to describe corn ("a Graine of marvelous great increase") and tobacco ("purgeth superfluous phlegm and other gross humours").

Historians regard Hariot's work as propaganda for Raleigh's effort to establish a colony in what he had named Virginia in honor of his "virgin queen," Elizabeth. John Smith and others soon added to his accounts.

The title page of Hariot's book describes its contents as "the commodities there found and to be raised, as well merchantable, as others for victuall, building and other necessarie uses for those that are and shalbe the planters there; and of the nature and manners of the naturall inhabitants." Hariot wanted to show the profit potential in a British settlement.

According to Hariot, his Roanoke Island colonists were "seated by Sir Richard Grenville, Knight, in the yeere 1585, which remained under the government of Ralph Lane, Esquire, one of her Majesty's Esquires..." Hariot and White, the artist, spent

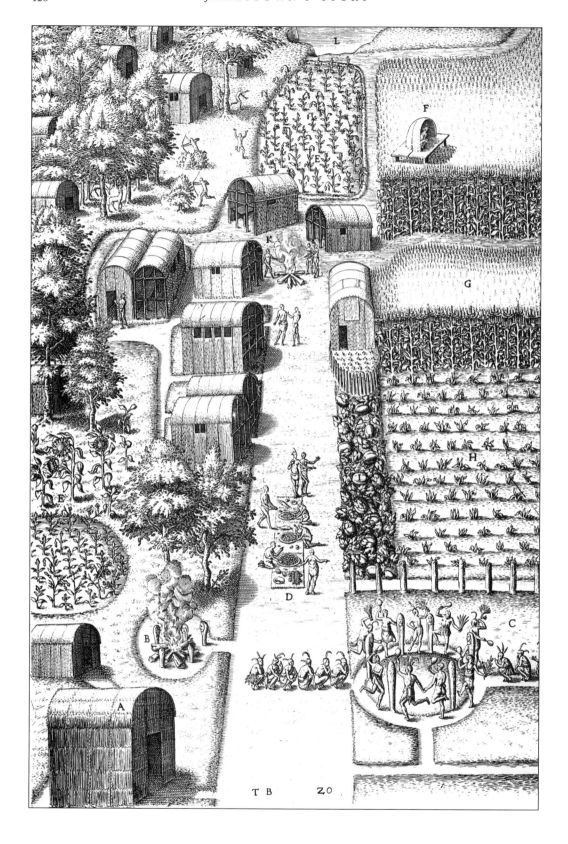

about 12 months in Virginia to make observations, then returned to London.

Hariot directed his book "to the Adventurers, Favourers, and Welwillers of the action, for the inhabiting and planting there." He included a list of potential Virginia exports that the British might sell: silk grass, silkworms, flax and hemp, alum, pitch, tar, resin, turpentine, sassafras, cedar, wine, walnut oil, marten furs, deerskins, civet cats (he does not say what use they might be, but promises "good profit"), iron, copper, pearls, sweet gum, and vegetable dyes.

He was impressed by "maize," which we call corn, used by the Indians to make bread and malt.

Hariot observed Indians living in groups of 10 or 12 houses near the coast. They were "clothed with loose mantles made of deerskin, and aprons of the same about their middles, all else naked." They have "no edge tools or weapons of iron or steel to offend us withal, neither know they how to make any." Their only weapons were bows and arrows, wood truncheons, and armor made of sticks.

Describing Indian warfare, Hariot wrote: "Their manner of wars amongst themselves is either by sudden surprising one another, most commonly about the dawning of the day, or moonlight; or else by ambushes, or some subtle devices. Set battles are very rare..."

As to religion, "They believe there are many Gods, which they call Mantoac, but different sorts and degrees; one only chief and great God, which hath been from all eternity."

Hariot concluded by urging settlers to leave England for new-found Virginia. He argued, "No Christian Prince hath any possession or dealing" there to contest Britain's claim to Virginia. He praised, "the excellent temperature of the air there in all seasons, much warmer than in England, and never so violently hot as sometimes [it] is under and between the Tropics."

Settlers could expect generous treatment from Sir Walter Raleigh, sponsor of the settlement, Hariot reported. "The least he has granted has been 500 acres to a man only for the adventure of his person." ❧

Newport News *Daily Press*, March 23, 1988

Facing page: Hariot wrote about various examples of Indian life including villages depicted in an engraving of a John White watercolor. (Engraved by Theodor de Bry from Thomas Hariot's **Admiranda Narratio fida tamen, de Commodis et Incolarum Ritibus Virginiae,** *Frankfurt, [1590])*

CHAPTER 24 ❦

Saving the Past

The blight of slavery that had sapped the economy of communities along the James River in the nineteenth century began to disappear in the decades after the Civil War. Railroads were run, banks chartered, cities were built, and public schools started.

Fortunately, in the rush to modernize, Virginia did not turn its back on its heritage at Jamestown, Williamsburg, and Yorktown. In fact, the Yorktown Centennial in 1881 marked a revival of interest in those colonial years.

After a seven-year cessation of classes, the College of William and Mary opened anew for students in 1888. And in 1889, Virginia women started a movement for restoration through their Association for the Preservation of Virginia Antiquities (APVA). This organization later helped the National Park Service and John D. Rockefeller, Jr., to save much of English America's first years along the James, from Carter's Grove westward to the mountains.

Appropriately enough, two Williamsburg-born women took the lead in alerting Americans to the decline of ancient sites, overlooked in the years of Civil War and Reconstruction. The two—Miss Mary Galt of Norfolk and Mrs. Cynthia Coleman of Williamsburg—were founders of the APVA, which today is the oldest statewide preservation organization in the nation.

Mary Galt's family had run the Williamsburg asylum in its early years. Cynthia Tucker Coleman was the great-granddaughter of St. George Tucker, well-known eighteenth-century Williamsburg lawyer. Both were energetic ladies who inspired their impoverished state to scrimp and save to keep cherished sites standing. Many others joined in.

It is hard to realize how miserably poor most Virginians were in the late 1880s and early 1890s. Wages for laborers were $1 per day. Professors taught for $1,000 a year. Meals were 15 cents and up. How could the APVA hope to save the historic sites without money?

The initial effort by the ladies was to rescue the colonial Williamsburg Powder Horn, now the Magazine, located on historic Duke of Gloucester Street in the middle of today's historic area. Mary Galt's Norfolk branch of the APVA raised most of the $400 needed for the purchase in 1889.

Additionally, businessmen and legislators agreed to help with other projects. The Commonwealth of Virginia in 1893 deeded to the APVA the old Jamestown church tower and adjoining church yard. Thereupon Mr. and Mrs. Edward E. Barney, who owned Jamestown Island, gave the organization an additional 22 acres surrounding the church. Later, the Old Dominion Land Company of Newport News gave the APVA the land surrounding the ruins of the colonial Capitol site in Williamsburg.

In early years, dues were $1 per year, but a few big spenders came to the ladies' aid. Major James Dooley, a former Confederate officer, gave $50, and "Officers of the C&O" gave $25. President Calvin Orcutt of the Newport News Shipyard gave $25, and Charles "Broadway" Rouss, a New York merchant born in Winchester, gave $5.

Feisty little Cynthia Coleman, twice widowed co-founder and for the first ten years director of the Williamsburg branch of the APVA, arranged "silver teas," bringing in donations of silver money. Other APVA chapters raised money by holding costume balls in colonial getup.

Fortunately the APVA found many friends. One was Mrs. Fitzhugh Lee, its first president, whose husband was then Virginia's governor and who was also a son of Gen. Robert E. Lee. Another friend was Lyon Gardiner Tyler, William and Mary's president and son of former U.S. President John Tyler.

Miss Mary Jeffery Galt of Norfolk (left) and Cynthia Beverley Tucker Coleman of Williamsburg were instrumental in the founding of the Association for the Preservation of Virginia Antiquities. Their first acquisition was at Jamestown. (Miss Galt from Mrs. V. Lee Kirby, and Mrs. Coleman from the Colonial Williamsburg Foundation)

In 1902 the APVA gained its best friend of all. He was the minister of Bruton Parish Church, Dr. William A. R. Goodwin. Invited to the church as minister to heal a bitter division in the congregation, he saw the need to preserve what was left of the colonial structure as well as all that still stood of colonial Williamsburg.

Many years later, after Dr. Goodwin had returned to Williamsburg and helped Dr. J. A. C. Chandler, William and Mary president, to expand the college, and persuaded John D. Rockefeller, Jr., to save Williamsburg, he tipped his hat to the handful of ladies who had met in Williamsburg to start the APVA. He wrote, "These devoted ladies bent like priestesses over the dying embers of ancient times and breathed upon them and made them glow again."

Reading the history of the APVA tells a lot about Tidewater in the 1880s. In those days, Virginians called frequently on wealthy Northerners to help save decrepit buildings, as Dr. Chandler and Dr. Goodwin were to do at William and Mary in the 1920s and '30s. From its 25-cents admission to the Powder Magazine, the APVA was able to hire a guide and to shore up the old building.

After the National Society of Colonial Dames in America, another historic heritage preservation organization, rebuilt Jamestown's brick church in the early 1900s, the Jamestown Exposition of 1907 speeded up the APVA's momentum. Branches

The sign at the APVA wrought iron main gate reads: "APVA Grounds. Admission 25 cents. Open Sunday, 1–5 p.m." The statue of Pocahontas facing up the James River stands near the path leading to the statue of Captain John Smith. This wrought-iron gate was relocated nearer the Old Tower Church prior to 1957. (From a post card published by B. E. Steel, Jamestown Island, Va., courtesy of Will Molineux)

General View of the A. P. V. A. Grounds
Jamestown Island, Virginia

Inside the entrance gate, several monuments can be seen between the river and the Old Tower Church. The statues of Pocahontas (foreground) and Captain John Smith (left background) are joined by a monument to the House of Burgesses, and the cross was erected by the Episcopal Church. (From a post card published by B. E. Steel, Jamestown Island, Va., courtesy of Will Molineux)

sprang up around Virginia, and landmarks, such as Mary Washington's Fredericksburg home, were acquired. Similar movements in other states awakened Americans, and restoration projects were born. Williamsburg's revival after 1926 and the start of the Colonial National Historical Park in Yorktown and Jamestown in the 1930s were evidence of preservationist zeal.

The APVA was a ladies' organization for its first 50 years, but men always lent a hand. Throughout the years, the organization acquired countless properties of all descriptions, preserving and protecting them. Today, the APVA owns nearly thirty properties across the Commonwealth and its good works are seen annually by millions of people—a far cry from its modest beginnings in Williamsburg and Jamestown. ⚜

The James—Where A Nation Began, The Dietz Press, Richmond, 1990

CHAPTER 25 ✻

Papers from 1600s Offer Insights

The libraries of the ancient English universities of Oxford and Cambridge continue to yield up long-lost documents about early Virginia and the other American colonies. A lot of these previously unnoticed papers were uncovered by researchers working on the restoration of Williamsburg, and other documents continue to turn up every now and then as historians explore musty British manuscripts of the 1600s.

The lost archive of the Virginia Company for 1619–1624—called the Ferrar Papers—was uncovered in the Old Library at Cambridge's Magdalene College by David Ransome, a historian from the Rhode Island School of Design.

The Virginia Company papers were found in the Samuel Pepys Library in the Pepys Building, the principal ornament of Magdalene College. (From Magdalene College, Cambridge University)

John Ferrar was the deputy to Sir Edwin Sandys, and early treasurer of the Virginia Company. Heads of companies were then called "treasurer" because they had the crucial job of keeping the company's money.

Ransome describes his findings in the spring 1996 edition of the *Virginia Magazine of History and Biography*. He says the first Jamestown settlers were not a bunch of losers, as they have been depicted, but were educated people of varied trades and talents. Thus, John Smith's Virginians were "not so unlike their more obviously bookish compatriots who sailed for New England in the following decades," Ransome writes.

The Virginia Company, represented by this seal, controlled the colony of Virginia from 1606 until its charter was revoked in 1624. (From Lyon G. Tyler, The Cradle of The Republic, *Richmond [1907])*

Perhaps it is because many top historians have been New Englanders that Virginia's settlers have often been depicted as godless gold-seekers, lacking the scholarly and industrious ways of the Pilgrims and Puritans.

Not so, says Ransome. "Many of them... must have been literate if the company thought an investment in instructional and devotional books worthwhile."

Ransome goes on to write that Virginia colonists were "more typical of England as a whole, rural as well as urban, the successful as well as the defeated."

Commenting on Ransome's findings, Dr. Karen Kupperman of New York University writes that "The Ferrar Papers offer... stunning re-evaluation of Virginia's founding years." She points out that the Virginia colony was created as a business venture to send gold, furs, and other products back to England. When the gold proved elusive, the Virginians turned to tobacco culture and land acquisition.

Ransome cites more than 500 Virginian documents in the Magdalene Library, where they have remained—until now—largely unread. They contain data on about 250 of the more than 3,000 people who "shipt... for Virginia" from 1619 to 1622. The papers describe the 57 women who sailed in 1621.

The Ferrar Papers list the average age of the men settlers at about 24 years, and 20 for the women. The passenger lists note the skills of the settlers, reflecting a more practical group than first landed at Jamestown in 1607. "The company was by 1619 avoiding the earlier mistake of including too many gentlemen," who had no work training, "and was sending over those who had skills that would immediately benefit the colony," Ransome says.

Among the settlers in 1619 were carpenters, blacksmiths, sawyers, bricklayers, masons, farmers, gardeners, laborers, sailors, millers, brewers, vintners, cooks, bakers, butchers, cutlers, grovers, tailors, chandlers, weavers, drapers, skinners, tanners, shoe-makers, glovers, goldsmiths and embroiderers. But the colony still attracted some "esquires" and "gentlemen."

Many settlers who arrived after 1619 came in family groups. The passenger list for the ship *Bona Nova* in that year included 90 people, at least 13 of whom were accompanied by kinfolk. A few came with their servants.

One married woman, Mrs. Mary White, came over in 1622 intending to join her husband Rev. Thomas White. However, he had already died. Adds Ransome, "But a shipboard acquaintance consoled the widowed Mrs. White and by the time of the 1625 muster, she was the wife of Isaac Champline."

In conclusion, Ransome writes that "the literacy and high educational level of the immigrants to new England have long been taken for granted. Now the careful record-keeping of the Ferrars also allows us to suggest that the Virginians were not as culturally far from their northerly compatriots as has been thought."

He cites several hundred books, both religious and practical, sent to Virginia by the Virginia Company. Among them were the Bible, the Anglican *Book of Common Prayer*, catechisms of the Anglican Church, and Bruen's "Pillgrimes Practise."

More practical books sent over dealt with raising mulberry trees for silkworms, cures for disease, and commodity rates.

Perhaps the underrating of Virginia's early settlers began in 1693 with England's Sir Josiah Child, who wrote in his *New Discourse on Trade* that "Virginia...[was] first peopled by a sort of loose land grant People, vicious and destitute of means to live at home, (being either unfit for Labour, or such as could find none to employ themselves about, or had so misbehaved themselves by Whoreing, thieving, or other Debauchery, that none would seet them to work.)"

So it is good to know our English ancestors were quality folk. 🜚

Newport News *Daily Press*, April 26, 1996

CHAPTER 26 ❧

Jamestown in 1907

J amestown in 1907 was quiet and similar in many ways to 1607. Much of the land was still forested and swampy, mosquitoes were frequent, and there were few "modern" intrusions.

However, down the James River at Norfolk, a World's Fair exposition was under way to celebrate the 300th anniversary of the English settlement of North America. The Jamestown Exposition, sponsored by the federal and Virginia state governments, cost a fortune, but it helped put Virginia's historic sites on the map.

In May 1993, few folks were alive to recall Jamestown as it was in 1907. One of them was Margaret Leal Work of McLean, whose grandfather was custodian for the Association for the Preservation of Virginia Antiquities at Jamestown. Mrs. Work,

A visiting congressional delegation from Washington, D.C. appointed to arrange for the tricentenary celebration of the settlement of Virginia visits the island prior to the 1907 event. (From a postal card by Raphael Tuck & Sons', Post Card Series NP2080, Landmarks of Virginia, courtesy of the editor)

The label said Jamestown Island "in 1907," but the photograph had to be taken before 1900 because a seawall was built in that location in 1900–1901 and the Jamestown Memorial Church was constructed in 1907 behind the existing seventeenth-century church tower. (From a postal card by Jamestown Amusement & Vending Co., Inc. of Norfolk for the 1907 Jamestown Exposition, courtesy of the editor)

who was nearly 100, remembered those years well and put her thoughts down in a letter with a sturdy script.

Her grandfather, William Leal, was a Richmond stonemason who came to Jamestown in 1907 to help erect the commemorative monument on the island. For a while, he and a daughter "roughed it," living in a temporary cabin. Later, when he was custodian for the APVA, he lived in the Yeardley House, which was built on the island at the time of the exposition.

"My father brought me there in 1907 for the Tricentennial," Mrs. Work reports, and "my parents and I lived in a tent for the two weeks we were there. After that the Yeardley House was built, and we had family reunions there every summer until Grandpa's death in 1915. Sometimes I stayed there all summer."

Jamestown then had a small public dock for freight and passenger steamers that every other day would traverse the James from Norfolk, Newport News, and Richmond and back. The 90 miles were covered in about 12 hours. There were also river boats—"day steamers" or "night steamers"—that also stopped at Jamestown, bringing the few tourists who ventured there.

To commemorate the 1607 settlement, the brick church tower of 1690 had been restored, and statues of John Smith and Pocahontas had been erected on the waterfront. Also during 1907, President Teddy Roosevelt's yacht, the *Mayflower*, tied up at the island dock, and there Lord James Bryce, British ambassador to the United

States, came ashore to make a speech at the dedication of the granite obelisk that still stands.

"Grandpa Leal was the postmaster, sheriff and tour guide," Mrs. Work recalls. "He sold postcards and a few souvenirs to tourists. People came by riverboat—the paddlewheeler *Pocahontas*—or by buggy or carriage from Williamsburg. Occasionally a motorcar came—not more than six to 10 visitors a week. There were no accommodations for visitors on the island or even for the work crew who built the monument and the sea wall."

While working near the church, Mrs. Work reports, "Grandpa unearthed a skeleton of a man...The graveyard was over-grown. Graves were covered with wood slabs. Names and dates were spelled out by short wood pegs hammered into the slabs."

About the same time, a U.S. Army engineer, Colonel Samuel Younge, came to build that first sea wall—a massive structure—designed to forever protect the island. While working on the project, Younge also discovered the early statehouse foundations and became so fascinated by Jamestown's archaeology that he stayed on to excavate more of the 22 acres of the island surrounding the brick church site. He apparently did not dig within the Confederacy's Civil War fort, laid up on the island in 1862. (Not until 1993 was an archaeological study of this area begun.)

Young Margaret enjoyed visiting her grandfather at Jamestown. "Often we found

The seventeenth-century church tower at Jamestown was still standing at the turn of the 20th century. (From the Library of Virginia, courtesy of the Rouse Collection, Earl Gregg Swem Library, College of William and Mary)

Indian beads, arrow heads, pieces of clay pipe, a Confederate or Union bullet, or cut stones that I was told were Indian good luck charms," she recalls.

"Light was by kerosene lamps. Windows were covered with cheesecloth, but gnats got through and swarmed around the lamps until they caught fire. Usually the lamps were thrown out the window aflame to prevent damage to the house."

Portions of the island at the church site had eroded after the capital of Virginia was removed from Jamestown in 1699. This nineteenth-century engraving shows the old Ambler plantation house at the far right. (From the Library of Virginia, courtesy of the Rouse Collection, Earl Gregg Swem Library, College of William and Mary)

Near the Yeardley House, Mrs. Work recalls, "there was a beautiful garden, originally patterned after the Rolfe garden in England. Chicken wire enclosed it." Later, deer that foraged over the island destroyed the garden. "A family of copperhead snakes lived under the house. I found one in my bed one night," she adds.

Mrs. Work writes, "We lived mostly on the land. Once a week we went to Williamsburg by horse and buggy, over what we called the back road—past the metal gates, over the wooden bridge without guard rails that crossed the back river (the Thoroughfare). It was a one-lane road. Trees met overhead from each side, so no sun came through. The thick yellow mud was hard to drive through, so the nine-mile trip could take three hours."

Williamsburg then was a muddy village of about 1,500 people, including about 300 William and Mary students, all male. "While the week's groceries were put in our wagon," Mrs. Work recalls, "we could buy ice cream or visit friends in town. That night and the next day we had fresh meat at Jamestown but could not keep it much longer. The river boat brought a 100 pound block of ice twice a week."

Henry Ford began to make Model Ts in 1908, and the first hard-surfaced road was run from Williamsburg to Jamestown about the same time. When cars began to come through, Mrs. Work remembers, "the trip to Williamsburg could be hazardous. The horse could panic and rear and gallop. Either the car or horse had to retreat to a side road." ☙

Newport News *Daily Press*, May 16, 1993

CHAPTER 27 ❧

The Jamestown Exposition

One of the memorable events of Virginia's history was the Jamestown Exposition of 1907, which introduced modern tourism to the reviving post-Civil War Virginia and celebrated the 300th anniversary of the start of English settlement at Jamestown.

The centerpiece of the extravaganza was in Norfolk at old Pine Beach—the name of the area then, but known as the Norfolk Naval Base now—and radiated across the water to Hampton, Newport News, Williamsburg, and Jamestown itself.

Excursion boats from all over the Chesapeake Bay, and from as far away as New York, brought people to the exposition, which in financial terms was a flop. But it gave Virginians a chance to boast of their history and it enabled many Americans to learn that the first permanent English settlement was at Jamestown, Virginia, in 1607, and not at Plymouth, Massachusetts in 1621.

It also made people of Tidewater conscious of their great future in tourism because of the historic sites, waterways, and bathing beaches that are there-abouts. Many hotels were built to accommodate visitors to the exposition, and new hard-surfaced roads were laid in the Jamestown and Williamsburg areas. Cars were just coming to the fore, and old postcards of the exposition grounds show a few of them amid the horse-drawn carriages.

Visitors gather at the Administration Building of the Jamestown Exposition on Norfolk's Sewell's Point where the navy base is now located. (From Amy Waters Yarsinske, Images of America—Jamestown Exposition, Imperialism on Parade, *Volume 1)*

History records the six-month exposition as a fiasco; it was never completed and was dogged by crisis.

An attractive Virginia congressman named Henry St. George Tucker—everybody called him "Harry"—was chairman of the exposition and managed to enlist federal support. But the star of the show was President Theodore Roosevelt, who visited the exposition and Jamestown, where he dedicated a monument that still stands.

Built by 21 state governments, majestic structures line Willoughby Boulevard and boardwalk, which faced the water. The Pennsylvania Building, depicting Independence Hall (left), and state homes (right) attracted thousands of visitors. (From Amy Waters Yarsinske, Images of America—Jamestown Exposition, Imperialism on Parade, Volume 1*)*

Lord James Bryce, British ambassador to the United States at the time, declared Jamestown the most important event in Anglo-Saxon history since the signing of the Magna Carta. Many people believed he was right.

Poor Harry Tucker's exposition was dogged by bad weather and a shortage of money. Some called it a failure. Despite round-the-clock construction in 1906, its ambitious brick expo buildings at Norfolk were unfinished on opening day

in the spring of 1907 and the expo was cruelly bad-mouthed.

Tucker and other sponsors were humiliated. The delay cut into attendance, resulting in a big deficit when the exposition closed.

But that did not bother children whose parents took them to Norfolk to see the foreign ships in the Raleigh Lagoon, to visit the exhibits in columned halls, and to ride the merry-go-round and enjoy other midway concessions. Parents from throughout Tidewater took their families to see the Exposition. Those Virginians who loved the expo cherished the exposition's souvenirs—commemorative plates, books, and postcards. Many households still have these keepsakes, which came to light in 1957, on the 350th Jamestown anniversary.

Most of the thirteen original states erected impressive "hospitality houses" along the waterfront; some of them remain on the Naval Base, reminders of the exposition long ago. The most elaborate and biggest was Pennsylvania's, a reproduction of Independence Hall, which later became the Officer's Club at the Naval Base and is now a naval museum.

Virginia House, adjacent to Pennsylvania's, is now the quarters of the Fifth Naval District commandant. In Missouri House many Atlantic fleet commanders have lived. These houses were built of brick and some had expensive columns and domes. Many states built museums to tout their achievements. There were also "palaces" of fine arts, commerce, and other areas, with all the grounds lighted at night by strings of incandescent bulbs.

The fun-and-games area of the exposition, aimed especially at children, was called "Powhatan's War Path." There stood the Oriental building, with camels, donkeys and bazaars. Another War Path show offered a sound-and-light reenactment of the Civil War battle of the *Merrimac* and *Monitor* that had taken place not far away in Hampton Roads on March 9, 1862.

Elsewhere on the War Path was "Princess Trixie," called "the educated horse," who "gives those wonderful exhibitions of intelligence which have made her famous on two continents," according to an old "official" photo album of the exposition.

And nearby was a simplified replica of the second colonial capitol at Williamsburg, which housed "The Burning of Jamestown," called "a strong amusement feature." The San Francisco earthquake, which had taken place a year earlier in 1906, was recalled in a pavilion called, "Destruction of San Francisco."

The expo created new rivalry between the Peninsula and Norfolk because residents of the Peninsula felt it should have been held at Jamestown or Williamsburg, instead of Norfolk. Historians say Norfolk was chosen because it had the transportation facilities, hotels, and money.

From Hampton Roads at the exposition, President Teddy Roosevelt sent off the "Great White Fleet" on its around-the-world trek. At the time, there also was a naval review with ships from the U.S. at an anchorage with four British warships, three Brazilian, two German, two Austrian, one Chilean, and one Argentine.

Representatives of 35 foreign nations gathered near Raleigh Lagoon, looking out from the Norfolk shore toward Hampton. There, Roosevelt reviewed a parade described as "the greatest military pageant witnessed in the South since the War between the States."

Sightseers from all along the East Coast thronged to Norfolk by train and boat for the festivities.

Amusement exhibitions and rides were found in the "War Path" area at the Exposition. Favorites were buildings featuring Paul Revere's ride, the Battle of Gettysburg, and the Battle of the **Merrimac** *and* **Monitor.** *(From Underwood and Underwood Stereoscopic Views)*

Trolleys and wagons conveyed travelers to the exposition that was laid out over 450 acres. Visitors trooped through pseudo-colonial exposition buildings.

After the exposition closed, its buildings lay idle and unused nearly 10 years,

A drawing in an advertisement for the Jamestown Exposition in 1907. (From the Mariners Museum, courtesy of the Rouse Collection, Earl Gregg Swem Library, College of William and Mary)

while creditors sought their money. As World War I loomed, Norfolk wisely sold the 450-acre exposition site to the federal government to become the biggest Navy facility in the nation. In fact, the government's holdings have expanded tenfold since 1917 and accommodate the Atlantic Fleet, Norfolk Naval Air Station and Supply Center.

As the base was developed, the exposition auditorium was converted to Naval Operations Base headquarters, and Raleigh Lagoon was filled in.

Today, little except the grand houses remains to recall the exposition. The wooden Pine Beach Hotel was demolished on the Naval Supply Center site. And the Friendship Arch given by Japan in 1907 for the area of the Raleigh Lagoon was torn down after Pearl Harbor was attacked in 1941.

The Jamestown Exposition showed a lot of people what great historic and scenic attractions Tidewater and Virginia had to offer. No wonder that not long afterwards property at Jamestown and Yorktown was bought by the federal government as part of the Colonial National Historical Park. And in 1926 John D. Rockefeller, Jr., was inspired to restore Williamsburg to its colonial appearance.

Yes, in spite of its financial losses, the Jamestown Exposition was a real success and provoked a number of activities that have enriched Virginia through the years. 🜨

Newport News *Daily Press*, September 15, 1991
and undated file notes

CHAPTER 28

Indians Were Really the Victims

Once, long ago, Native Americans—Indians—were the enemy from the perspective of the English settlers. Now, as Americans have come to appreciate their heritage, Indians are held in esteem.

That fact was clearly demonstrated in the summer of 1995 at Jamestown Island [now run by the U.S. National Park Service and the Association for the Preservation of Virginia Antiquities] and at Jamestown Settlement (the state-run historical interpretive museum) where record crowds showed up to learn about Pocahontas, the Indian princess whose story was told most recently by Walt Disney in a commercially successful, but woefully historically inaccurate, animated movie.

Scholars such as James Axtell at the College of William and Mary and Helen Rountree, formerly at Old Dominion University, are studying the lives of the Native Americans. These studies have revealed that Powhatan's tribes were not the wanton murderers we once thought, but a relatively peaceable society of farmers, fishermen and hunters. Tidewater was the Indians' stomping ground. These Algonquians were the forest-dwellers who confronted Captain John Smith and others in 1607.

By the time Europeans began to settle North America, Indians were scattered along the Atlantic from Canada to Florida in the form of major tribal groupings. As the Europeans learned more about them, they assigned the various tribes to Indian "nations," depending on the Indian dialect they spoke. Powhatan's people belong to the Algonquian nation, speaking a dialect in common with others along the Atlantic Coast.

The Indians who lived farther inland in Virginia belonged to different nations that sometimes warred with the Powhatans for hunting ranges or for status or even for women as war trophies.

Algonquian women raised vegetables to provide about 70 percent of their food: corn, squash, beans, pumpkins, and other edibles. Then the women cooked food in clay pots, a few of which still survive. They also gathered nuts, roots and berries. That left the men free to fish and hunt, which furnished the remainder of their food. Deer meat was a favorite, along with oysters, crabs and various fish. Large oyster shell deposits along the York and other Virginia rivers have helped identify onetime Indian village sites.

No views of Indian villages at the time of Jamestown exist, but John White, who accompanied one of the Roanoke voyages, made some watercolor drawings of villages near there. This is the palisade of the Indian town of Pomeiooc. (Engraved by Theodor de Bry from Thomas Hariot's Admiranda Narratio fida tamen, de Commodis et Incolarum Ritibus Virginiae, *Frankfurt, [1590])*

A few buffaloes from the western mountains found their way to eastern Virginia, where the Powhatans hunted them for their skins and meat. Scholars tell us the Indians roamed to find food and furs and also to claim maidens from other tribes as wives. It seems that the Indians were aware of the folly of inbreeding with cousins, and young males like to claim their mates from enemy tribes.

Children matured early. Girls "married" at about age 12 and boys at about age 14. They absorbed adult skills and lore as they grew up, living in long houses built of saplings, covered with skins or with matted reeds and bark. In each house lived from six to 20 family members. Powhatan's villages, showed on an early John Smith map of Virginia, ranged from 30 to 600 people.

Having little metal for implements, Powhatan's people lived the low-tech life of Stone Age people around the globe, fabricating tools from wood and stone, and making roofing of bark, clothes from animal skins, and needles and fishhooks from bones.

Students of Indian lore tell us that Powhatan's people spent about five hours a day working, leaving plenty of time for sociability and worship. Their chief god was Oke, who punished wrongdoers. Only Indian chiefs and priests learned the primary rituals and secrets of religion, leaving tribesmen of lower status to worship at simple ceremonies in a ring of carved ceremonial posts.

Powhatan's Indians were relatively unwarlike. After all, they had plenty of fish and oysters to eat, plus abundant wild game—until the arrival of the English when their herds of deer and other animals had to been shared with John Smith and gun toting hunters. Warfare, however, was occasional between the Powhatans and their Piedmont and Southwest Virginia neighbors, who belonged to the Siouian-speaking tribes called Monacans (the Goochland County town of Manakin is named for them), and the Manohoacs. Warfare was brought on by droughts and other phenomena that reduced the food supply.

Powhatan and his successors held life and death powers over tribesmen, demanding frequent tribute of corn and other edibles. He was said to have had more than 100 wives. The principal chief moved from one village to another, seeking comfort and fish and game in season. A favorite village of Powhatan—Cantaunkack—lay on the north shore of the York in present Gloucester County. It was later called Shelly—for its mounds of shells left by the Indians.

Historians estimate the Powhatan people were in Virginia more than 1,000 years before the English arrived. They had their ups and downs, for droughts and epidemics assailed them. But about 15,000 of the Powhatans once lived in villages along the Virginia-Carolina-Maryland coastal plain.

The planting in Virginia of Spanish tobacco about 1610 was one of the worst things to happen to the Indians. Its popularity in England led to the rapid spread of tobacco farms, the importation of slaves, and inevitably the pressure of Englishmen to force the Indians out of Tidewater. Many Virginia Indians fled north and took up with Iroquois. Some of their descendants may survive in Indian reservations at Salamanca, New York, and elsewhere around the Great Lakes.

On late sixteenth-century tobacco labels the Virginia Indians were portrayed in an offensive way. Little dignity was held for them. (From Ingham Foster Collection, Imperial Tobacco Company, Bristol, England)

Other Indians intermarried with black or white people and lost their genetic identity. Still others accepted life on the Mattaponi and Pamunkey Indian reservations, created in 1658 near the present town of West Point in King William County, where their descendants live lives that combine commuting, small farming, and fishing.

Virginia's Indians received a poor bargain from the Commonwealth when the reservations were established. They received little except their land, a pittance compared with the elaborate benefits granted by the federal government later to the Plains Indians out West.

One of the few Indian customs to survive is the practice of the Mattaponi and Pamunkey to make gifts, in the form of deer, wild turkey or other game, to the Governor of Virginia at Thanksgiving.

In retrospect, the Indians were not truly America's "enemies." They were more truly its victims. ☙

Newport News *Daily Press*, April 7, 1996 and December 9, 1990

CHAPTER 29 ❧

Pocahontas Will Remain in England

Singer Wayne Newton, who has made a career of his Las Vegas nightclub acts, visited Jamestown some years ago and expressed the hope in a television interview that the body of Pocahontas could be brought from England and reburied. He is interested because he thinks he descends from that Virginia Indian.

Newton's proposal carried a special interest, because Virginia hoped to do exactly that in 1957 during the 350th anniversary of the first permanent English settlement in the New World. But it was impossible. The Indian princess' remains lie unidentified in the large burial ground around St. George's Church at Gravesend, England. No one knows which grave is hers because she was buried in an undesignated site in 1617, and many others have been interred there since.

But it is a romantic notion, and Newton cannot be blamed for getting excited

Pocahontas with her husband, John Rolfe, at the court of James I of England during their visit to London in 1614. (From a postal card by Jamestown Amusement & Vending Co., Inc. of Norfolk for the 1907 Jamestown Exposition, courtesy of the editor)

about it. The Norfolk singer-entertainer visited Jamestown three times within a five-year span.

It takes a trip to faraway Gravesend to realize the impossibility of bringing Pocahontas "home" to Virginia, as was first proposed back during the Jamestown Exposition in 1907. When visiting that industrial town beside the Thames in 1956 on a commemorative visit with Governor Thomas B. Stanley and 105 other Virginians, we learned how little is known about where the Indian princess is buried.

Her husband, Jamestown colonist John Rolfe, took Pocahontas to England in 1616 on a trip to renew ties with his family living there. It also was an effort to publicize the struggling Virginia settlement and to promote the sale in England of Virginia tobacco. Rolfe had begun about 1612 to profit from his shipment to London of tobacco grown from seed he had obtained with the aid of a ship captain.

One of the most popular figures in American history, Pocahontas was the daughter of Chief Powhatan. She had befriended Captain John Smith (Smith wrote that she saved his neck from her father's warriors), and had been baptized as Rebeckah.

In April 1614, Pocahontas married Rolfe, a young widower who was to lose his life in the Indian uprising in 1622, when nearly a third of the 1,200 English colonists in Virginia were wiped out.

In 1956 Gravesend contained little of its seventeenth-century character except for St. George's Church. At a small Gravesend inn on the river, where we lunched, a traffic sign advised vehicles to "Please Park Pretty," meaning close to the curb. The original Anglican church, small but romantic, has lost most parishioners to death and the suburbs.

This portrait is apparently a mid-eighteenth century painting of Indian Princess Pocahontas, derived from an engraving by Dutch master Simon van de Passe, done while she was visiting England in 1616. (From the Rouse Collection, Earl Gregg Swem Library, College of William and Mary)

How does Pocahontas happen to be buried in this remote place? It is a poignant story.

After being presented by Lady De la Warr, wife of Virginia's governor, at the court of King James I, the Indian princess had excitedly encountered her old Jamestown friend, John Smith (romantics say she loved him, not Rolfe), and then journeyed with her husband and infant son, Thomas, to Gravesend to board ship to return to Virginia. Alas, she sickened there and died before the ship sailed. Her husband buried her at Gravesend.

A grieving Rolfe returned to Virginia in 1617. Harvard historian John Fiske believed that Rolfe married Pocahontas not for love, but as a calculated move to gain Powhatan's favor. However, most of us like to think he was genuinely in love, as he wrote Virginia's governor that he was when he sought official permission to marry the Christianized Indian in the Church of England. Pocahontas' son became the forefather of many Virginians when his daughter Jane married a member of the prominent Bolling family.

(*Editor's note:* While Pocahontas

St. George's Church at Gravesend had stood for 120 years when Pocahontas was buried in its graveyard in 1617. The church was destroyed by fire in 1726 and was replaced by this building. (From Paul Relf for the rector and parish, St. George's Church, Gravesend, England)

was in England in 1616, an engraving of her was produced by the Dutch engraver Smion van de Passe. Many subsequent portraits of her apparently were based largely or in part on the de Passe engraving. An oil painting, (which appeared by 1760-1770) of the Indian princess by an unknown eighteenth century artist, hung for years, in Booton Hall, the English ancestral home of her husband - John Rolfe. Later, it was purchased by Andrew Melton, a major American art collector, and hangs now in the National Portrait Gallery in Washington. A copy of that painting, commissioned in the early 1890s by Henry S. Wellcome was presented to the United States Senate in 1899. Another contemporary copy was given by Paul Mellon to the Jamestown-Yorktown Foundation, now exhibited at Jamestown Settlement and yet another copy is in the Virginia state capitol.) ⚜

Newport News *Daily Press*, August 19, 1990

CHAPTER 30

Chief Powhatan's Mantle

One of the earliest remnants of Britain's settlement at Jamestown in 1607 returned to that James River site in 1990 on loan from Oxford's Ashmolean Museum. It is a deerskin mantle decorated with seashells, long exhibited in England as "Powhatan's Habit."

The Virginia Indian object was acquired by Oxford through gift from London scholar and antiquarian Elias Ashmole in 1683. Presumably it was taken from Jamestown to London by a returning Englishman and has been a celebrated curiosity at Oxford for more than 300 years.

The decorated mantle, composed of four skins sewn together, was long assumed to have been given by Chief Powhatan to Virginia's English settlers, but the Oxford museum no longer makes that claim. According to historian James Axtell, an Indian authority at the College of William and Mary, "This is probably the most outstanding seventeenth-century artifact in eastern North America."

Historians conclude that the Algonquians had been living in Virginia at least 1,000 years before the arrival of the English settlers, though some anthropologists suggest a much earlier date on the basis of archaeological findings. Originally, the Powhatans had been wide-ranging hunters who fished in Tidewater each summer and moved inland to hunt

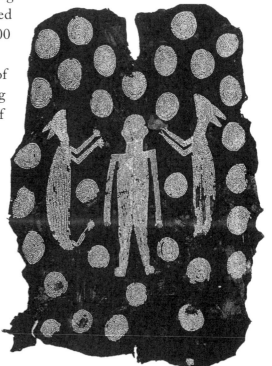

This deerskin decorated with figures made of shells is believed by some to be the ceremonial cloak of Chief Powhatan. It was taken to England in the 1600's. (From the Ashmolean Museum, Oxford University, courtesy of the Rouse Collection, Earl Gregg Swem Library, College of William and Mary)

deer and other wildlife in winter. However, the tribesmen had grown into a settled agricultural society by the 1500s.

"Powhatan's habit" is thought to have been owned by a chief or high priest, who may have worn it or may have hung it in an Indian long-house used as a temple. These structures were made by the Algonquians of bent saplings, tied with deerskin thongs to create arches that could be covered with removable thatch blinds which rolled up in summer to permit ventilation. [These structures were depicted in John White's Roanoke illustrations of 1585.]

"Powhatan's mantle," as it is also called, seemed well preserved when on exhibit. It is decorated with shells sewn on with animal sinews. Around a central human figure are two four-legged animals of uncertain idenity.

The Ashmolean Museum also exhibits other early Virginia objects collected by pioneer English naturalist

This is the only known depiction of Chief Powhatan, in an engraving from Captain John Smith's map. (From The Generall Historie of Virginia, New-England, and the Summer Isles, *[1624])*

John Tradescant II (the younger) on three or more voyages to Virginia in its first half-century. Tradescant is known to have visited Edward Digges, a pioneer York River planter, who lived on the present site of the Yorktown Naval Weapons Station. From his voyages, Tradescant sent back to England countless Virginia plants and stuffed birds and animals.

It was Tradescant's "Closett of Rarities" in London that Elias Ashmole acquired on the explorer's death and ultimately gave to Oxford. Whether Tradescant himself acquired the Powhatan mantle in Virginia is unknown, but historians now agree that it is authentic early Virginia Indian handiwork. 🦋

Newport News *Daily Press*, March 18, 1990

CHAPTER 31 ✣

Indian Villages
Reveal Histories

Of all Powhatan's many villages, the seventeenth-century Indian chieftain preferred Cantaunkack on the Gloucester Shore of the York River. Its attraction was rich beds of oysters and fertile soil for corn and beans.

This spot is so full of Indian artifacts that Virginia's Department of Historic Resources excavated it for two years, 1987–1989. A report on the work was published in the summer 1990 edition of the department's *Notes on Virginia*.

The area—roughly opposite where the Yorktown Naval Weapons Station is located today—is known as Shelly, a former Page family enclave at the confluence of the York and Carter's Creek. Native Americans occupied this shore for at least 1,000 years before English settlers claimed the area in the 1600s. The digs revealed about 30 prehistoric and historical archaeological sites within a 176-acre tract, now listed on the National Register of Historic Places as Shelly Archaeological District.

There are several theories on how the Algonquian Indians came to Tidewater, but by the time the settlers arrived at Jamestown in 1607, the Algonquians numbered about 9,000 people in an agrarian society divided into 32 tribes.

Powhatan's tribesmen occasionally warred with the Monacan and Manahoac tribes of central Virginia, who belonged to the more warlike Sioux nation. They fought not for land, but for status, for women, and for the chance to trade with other Indians.

In their Gloucester excavations, archaeologists found a layer of oyster shells dating from about 300 to 900 years A.D. According to archaeologists Anthony Opperman and Dr. E. Randolph Turner III, "Shelly represents one of the largest and best preserved surviving examples of this important Native American site type."

The site of Cantaunkack is depicted on a map sent by John Smith to England in 1608. Indian trader William Claiborne also mentioned the location in 1629, when he wrote that he landed there "and fought ye Indians and cut down their corn."

"The remarkably well-preserved deposits include intact living floors" and other features, the Opperman and Turner report said.

The archaeologists found small campsites, evidently used by prehistoric nomads from as early as 3,000 B.C. "As such," Opperman and Dr. Turner wrote, "they provided important information on settlement patterns over the landscape and on how seasonal use of Shelly changed over time... These changes apparently are related to rising population" and a more settled lifestyle.

The Algonquians' reign at Shelly ended in 1639, when the English crown granted the property to George Menefie, member of the Governor's Council and Jamestown merchant. Menefie's grant of 3,000 acres was the first Gloucester land to be given to an English settler. It remained in the Menefie family until 1680, when it was acquired by John Mann and eventually passed, by marriage, to the great colonial Page family.

Another well-known Indian village was Kiskiak, located between King's Creek and Felgate's Creek, in the picturesque wooded area now part of the Naval Weapons Station in York County and now traversed by a bridge of the Colonial Parkway.

The English took over Kiskiak about 15 years after settling Jamestown and it became the northern point of a stockade erected across the Peninsula to protect them against Powhatan's people. The stockade extended from Felgate's Creek and Kiskiak south to a point west of Jamestown on the James.

The settlers soon converted "Kiskiak" to "Chiskiak," which came to be spelled

The late James Ware, a member of the Rappahannock tribe, looked over a display of animal pelts and baskets and an old dugout canoe in the Indian Lodge at Jamestown Festival Park in the late 1950s. (From the collection of the Jamestown-Yorktown Foundation, photo by Thomas L. Williams)

and pronounced by some as "Cheesecake." The pre-1607 occupants of the area were the Kiskiak tribe, one of the member tribes of the Powhatan confederacy. After the massacre of settlers in 1622, William Claiborne drove the Kiskiaks across the York River into Gloucester, near where Powhatan lived at Cantaunkack. Settlers began to claim land grants along the York, and settlements centered at Kiskiak and York village, now called Yorktown. Because of the proximity to Gloucestertowne directly across the river, Yorktown survived and became a county seat, while Kiskiak today is merely a name in history.

One of the first Kiskiak settlers was Edward Digges whose later "York River sweet-scented" tobacco was prized by London buyers. The Digges' family called their plantation Bellfield and foundations of one Bellfield house were excavated and examined in the 1930s and still lie underground today just off the Colonial Parkway.

Edward Digges was a naturalist and friend of John Tradescant, the younger, a colorful London collector of fauna and flora, who came to Virginia three or four times in its infancy, staying with Digges.

(*Editor's note:* In the late spring of 2003, Dr. Turner, a regional director of the Virginia Department of Historic Resources, announced another archaeological find, which could outdistance the others in historical importance. It is Werowocomoco, Chief Powhatan's principal village and home of the Indian Princess Pocahontas. It was here, according to an account by Captain John Smith, that Pocahontas saved his life.

Located in Gloucester County off Purton Bay on the York River, the Native American site is today the farm of Lynn and Bob Ripley. Dr. Turner told reporters proudly, "Literally, the arrow points right here." Thousands of artifacts already have been recovered, including a vast number of arrowheads, spear points and pieces of pottery.

A number of the artifacts are from the "late woodland" and "contact" periods, just prior to and after the founding of Jamestown. Native American artifacts also dating to 1000 B.C. also have been uncovered.

Archaeologists hope that future excavations will uncover the layout of the village and will provide information on the trade among Indian villages and with the early English settlers.

"While the association of Werowocomoco with Jamestown is indeed important, for us it really represents something far more," Dr. Turner told the media. "Here we're talking about the culmination of over 15,000 years of Native Americans living in what today we call Virginia.") ❧

Newport News *Daily Press*, August 1, 1990 and September 9, 1990

CHAPTER 32 ✤

Wolstenholm Towne— A Discovery

Lost towns are romantic, and every several years Virginia discovers another, often through laborious efforts of field archaeologists. One of the most exciting discoveries of seventeenth century Virginia was the finding of an early settlement—Wolstenholm Towne—a village on the James about eight miles downstream from Jamestown. Unlike the colony's capital, Wolstenholm was wiped out in the Indian uprising of 1622.

Wolstenholm was a primitive, palisaded settlement near the present Carter's Grove mansion in James City County, one of the colony's eight original shires. The village was accidentally discovered in 1970 by an archaeological team under the direction of Ivor Noël Hume from Colonial Williamsburg, who at the time was seeking remains of early Carter's Grove outbuildings. What they found were a series of structures within a palisade and other homes outside the area along with the long-lost skeletons of men, women and children who died cruelly in the massacre.

Since discovery, Wolstenholm Towne has become internationally known. It was the subject of an article by Noël Hume in the *National Geographic* magazine and of a book by him, *Martin's Hundred*, published by Alfred Knopf in 1982. It also has been the subject of several television documentaries.

Wolstenholm Towne of the seventeenth century lay

The first layers of soil have been scraped away revealing the post holes for the fort at Wolstenholm Towne, five or six miles down river from Jamestown. Notice the four large holes for a watch-tower in the center forefront. (Photo by Ivor Noël Hume)

within an English land grant in James City called Martin's Hundred. Most of the land was later absorbed in the Burwell family's plantation, called Carter's Grove.

A highway marker at the entrance to Carter's Grove reads: "Martin's Hundred: On both sides of this road and extending west was the plantation known as Martin's Hundred, originally 80,000 acres. Settled in 1619, this hundred sent delegates to the first legislative assembly in America, 1619. In the Indian uprising of 1622, 78 persons were slain here."

Among the more interesting artifacts uncovered at Wolstemholm Towne was a helmet from the early seventeenth century. An archaeologist carefully works with the helmet during the excavation process. (Photo by Ivor Noël Hume)

Noël Hume and his archaeological team came across skeletons of Wolstenholm residents lying as they fell when attacked by the Indians long ago. In several cases tomahawks had pierced their skulls and their scalps removed. Other archaeological investigations uncovered the palisade itself and shadows of the houses and buildings constructed within it. Today, visitors can visit a major archaeological museum on the Wolstenholm discoveries, walk the site and understand the people who lived here.

Wolstenholm was typical in its brief and tragic history of most of the dozen or so settlements then established along the James by colonists who came to Jamestown and as it grew moved to form their own settlements. In 1619 there were 11 of these "particular plantations" that elected delegates to the first assembly. They included Argall's Gift, where the James City County community of First Colony now stands; Flowerdieu Hundred in Prince George County; Lawne's plantation in a wilderness area on the river shore in Isle of Wight County; and Martin's Brandon in Prince George, where Brandon plantation now stands.

Another "particular plantation" was Berkeley in Charles City County. A little-known settlement area was Archer's Hope on the James, at the mouth of College Creek, where a small seaport once stood with several structures, now long gone. 🕸

The James—Where A Nation Began, Dietz Press, Richmond, 1990

The outline of the fort at Wolstenholm Towne was found during an archaeological dig and recon-structed by the Colonial Williamsburg Foundation to show visitors how the area looked about 1622. The watchtower has been rebuilt on the left. (Photo by Ivor Noël Hume)

Costumed interpreters at Wolstenholm Towne are engaged in the final work on the reconstructed watchtower. (Photo by Ivor Noël Hume)

CHAPTER 33

The Jamestown Festival of 1957

T he Jamestown Festival of 1957, celebrating America's 350th birthday, was a joint project of the U.S. government and the Commonwealth of Virginia. Unlike the celebration 50 years earlier that was centered in Norfolk, this event was held on Jamestown Island and on nearby state property.

President Dwight D. Eisenhower led Americans in commemorating the English settlement. "It is important for us to call to memory the great achievements of our forefathers in hewing out of the wilderness a new nation. The founding of the first

Jamestown Festival Park grounds shortly after it opened in April 1957. This state-operated facility was built on the nearby mainland to commemorate the 350th anniversary of the settlement of Jamestown. (From the collection of the Jamestown-Yorktown Foundation)

Three full-scale reproductions of the ships that transported the settlers from England to Virginia—the Susan Constant, Godspeed *and* Discovery—*are moored at Jamestown Settlement. (Photo courtesy of the Jamestown-Yorktown Foundation)*

permanent English settlement in 1607 at Jamestown, Virginia (and) the establishment there of the first representative form of government in the New World... are important milestones in our nation's history."

The focal point for the state's commemoration of Jamestown was Jamestown Festival Park, a historical exhibit of the first permanent British settlement overseas.

Here in an arc of new buildings, daily programs were presented to freshen American's memory of the men who established Jamestown. In front of the buildings was a large field—the Mall—site of pageantry, ceremonials, parades, public addresses, music and drama, exhibits of art and history and entertainment.

During the Festival year, President Eisenhower visited the Park as did Queen Elizabeth II of Great Britain and numerous other foreign dignitaries and VIPs.

The main buildings included an Information Center, designed to resemble an Indian lodge and the Old World and New World Pavilions. The British government sponsored, "The Old World Heritage," a major exhibit in the Old World Pavilion, while the "New World Achievement" exhibit, presented by the Commonwealth of Virginia chronologically followed the British display.

Elsewhere in the park was Powhatan's Lodge, a reconstruction of a ceremonial lodge of the Indians who populated the area around Jamestown in 1607. The lodge closely followed the depiction in John Smith's map of Virginia and was 36 feet long and 16 feet wide. It was framed of saplings, tied with rawhide, and covered with mats of cattails, woven together with hemp thread. The adjacent dance circle was copied from the water color drawings of John White, who painted the Indians of the North Carolina coast 20 years before the Jamestown settlement.

Cover design of a brochure for the 1957 Jamestown Festival commemoration featuring the entranceway with the main building designed to resemble an Indian lodge. (Courtesy of the editor)

At a pier in the nearby James River, full-scale reconstructions of the *Susan Constant*, *Godspeed* and *Discovery* were moored. The reconstructions were based on extensive research conducted in the records of the British Admiralty and in the famous collection of Samuel Pepys, a clerk in the Admiralty in the reigns of Charles II and James II.

A few hundred yards away was the James Fort, a carefully detailed reconstruction of the first settlers' fort with its main entrance from the river side. It was of a triangular design, just as colonist George Percy wrote in 1607. It had "three Bulwarkes, at every corner, like a halfe moone, and foure or five pieces of artillerie mounted in them." In the center of the fort stood the church, guardhouse and storehouse. Paralleling each of the three sides was "a fair row of houses."

(*Editor's note*: Portions of the original 1607 fort were uncovered during a major archaeological investigation of Historic Jamestowne by archaeologists for the APVA Preservation Virginia. The shape of the fort and houses inside was found to be somewhat different from the accepted views in the 1950's.)

Adjacent to the Festival Park and just across the isthmus from the island was the glasshouse exhibit, sponsored by the National Park Service, and design to pay tribute to "America's first factory." Unsuccessful in their efforts to find instant wealth in

Through the years, visitors to Jamestown Festival Park, now called Jamestown Settlement, have had the opportunity to see daily demonstrations by costumed interpreters showing how the Jamestown settlers lived.
These photographs are from the 1980s. (Courtesy of the Jamestown-Yorktown Foundation)

1607, the settlers in 1608 set up a glass furnace on the shores of the James, a mile from Jamestown, and attempted to make glass from the coarse river sand. After producing briefly in 1608 and 1609, the enterprise apparently lapsed until it was briefly revived in 1620.

In 1931, the remains of the 1608 furnace were discovered and identified. Since that time, leaders in the glass industry have succeeded in creating the Jamestown Glasshouse Foundation and in raising more than $100,000 from glass workers and companies to assist the Park Service in creating the Glasshouse exhibit. ❧

The Jamestown Festival Official Program, 1957

CHAPTER 34 ❧

Queen Elizabeth II at Jamestown

The Queen of England finally visited her "Virginia."

The Colony was named in the late sixteenth century for Queen Elizabeth, the virgin queen, but it had to wait more than 350 years for a royal visit, this time, by the second Queen Elizabeth. The first settlement was founded during the reign of James I.

(*Editor's note*: As executive director of the Jamestown Festival in 1957, Parke Rouse Jr. participated in many of the activities and events that culminated in the visit by the British monarch. This is a personal reminiscence.)

It was 1956 when I went to London with [Virginia] Governor Thomas Stanley, Del. Lewis McMurran of Newport News, the legislator heading the event and other Virginians to invite the queen to come Virginia to celebrate the 350th anniversary of the settlement of Jamestown.

I know it's name-dropping but queens aren't everyday occurrences in an American's life. When Stanley received the call from Buckingham Palace inviting the Stanleys, McMurrans and Rouses to meet the queen, my wife and Edith McMurran got out their white gloves and practiced curtsies. The invitation specified cocktail party dresses for ladies

The Duke of Edinburgh and Queen Elizabeth II pause in Jamestown Festival Park to view a marker that commemorates the 350th anniversary of the English "overseas expansion." (From the Newport News **Daily Press***)*

and "lounge suits" for men, although our audience was at 11:30 a.m.

U.S. Ambassador to the Court of St. James, Winthrop Aldrich, escorted the Stanleys to the palace in his limousine. The McMurrans and Rouses tagged along in another limousine. At the palace gates we encountered a throng (await-ing Princess Margaret we learned later), the ladies ack-nowledged their huzzas by waving regally.

The queen's Scottish guards in kilts helped us out of the cars. In the palace, we were greeted by Sir John Hope and a lady-in-waiting, who turned out to be Somerset Maugham's daughter. The Aldriches warmly introduced us, and her ladyship asked if we knew how to bow or curtsy. Of course we did.

We were ushered into the reception room that had hearth fires glowing at each end and a glorious garden outside French doors that lined one side of the room. Suddenly the queen's

Queen Elizabeth II and Virginia Governor Thomas B. Stanley watch as Indian interpreter Lou Ethel Trickett demonstrates the traditional way to grind maize during a 1957 tour of Jamestown Festival Park. (From the Virginia Gazette, *photo by Merritt Ierley)*

equerry, Sir Patrick Plunket, said the queen was ready to receive the Virginia group.

The Aldriches went first and then stood by while Elizabeth II, very young and a little nervous and who had succeeded to the throne only four years earlier, eyeballed each of us as we stepped forward and curtsied or bowed.

The conversation was awkward because amid all of the pomp and ceremony we were going through we could never bring up the subject of an invitation to Virginia. Protocol prevented such a thing because only the president can invite a foreign head of state to the United States, but we could tell her about Virginia's celebration the next year and remind her that it was the beginning of England's overseas empire. Gov. Stanley did express a hope that she'd come to Virginia.

Things brightened a bit when the queen pointed through the window at a high-rise being built behind the palace. "My children will have no privacy," she lamented. We chuckled sympathetically, but we were relieved when the queen turned to Plunket and said, "Patrick, will you press the buzzer?"

The electrified doors then opened for us to make our bows and depart. I could take a deep breath again. It had been only 20 minutes.

Our departure from the palace brought us more huzzas from the crowd still

Queen Elizabeth II and the Duke of Edinburgh leave the **Susan Constant,** *one of the three reconstructed ships, at Jamestown Festival Park during their 1957 visit. (From the Newport News* **Daily Press***)*

standing at the gates. "They think we're royalty," Edith McMurran said to my wife, Betsy. The next day, the *Times of London* and the *Telegram* reported the queen's calandar, noting that she had received us. Names and everything.

When Queen Elizabeth and Prince Philip came to Jamestown 18 months later—in October 1957—the queen and I eyeballed each other again as she made a tour through Festival Park, inspecting various aspects including the reconstructed James Fort and the three ships. The queen was a serious sightseer and took in everything, reading labels and listening to guides all afternoon long.

For sentimental reasons I most enjoyed seeing Elizabeth standing on the shore where John Smith and his fellow voyagers had landed in 1607 to claim Virginia for the English crown. The queen came to Jamestown for that reason. It was the most exciting day of my life.

Prince Philip very much enjoyed boarding the *Susan Constant* and stayed so long that the procession fell behind its schedule. The queen apologized for that in a wifely way, explaining that she couldn't do a thing with him when he went aboard a ship.

The royals were especially interested in the Powhatan Lodge and its Indian guides—depicting the way and the life of the natives at the time of the English settlement.

Later that afternoon the queen visited the College of William and Mary and Colonial Williamsburg. The day concluded with a black-tie reception in Williamsburg and by 10:30 a.m. the next day Her Majesty Elizabeth, by the grace of God, Queen of England, Defender of the Faith, etc., had left.

(*Editor's note:* Queen Elizabeth returned to Jamestown 50 years later on May 4, 2007, for the 400th anniversary celebration of the James-town settlement. Initially she was welcomed by U.S. Vice President Richard Cheney, then state and local officials, and they toured the newly rebuilt facilities at Jamestown Settle-ment [called Jamestown Festival Park when she visited in 1957].

Sam Robinson, interpreter at the Jamestown church tower, talks with Queen Elizabeth II and the Prince Philip, Duke of Edinburgh, in the graveyard outside the church. (From Rouse Collection, Earl Gregg Swem Library, College of William and Mary, photo by the Association for the Preservation of Virginia Antiquities)

Accompanied by Prince Philip, Duke of Edinburgh, she visited the reconstructed James Fort while the prince looked at three ships moored nearby. The royal couple accepted gifts at dockside. Then the queen quickly traveled to the adjacent Jamestown Island where archaeologists have been busy for a decade, uncovering remains of the early English set-tlement at Historic Jamestowne, including the original fort.

The queen expressed interest in seventeenth-century arti-facts uncovered at the site, stopping at the elaborate archae-ology museum and then visiting current digging at the fort site. She told William and Mary students later that day that she felt like "Rip Van Winkle" during her brief visit, which again included stops at the college and Colonial Williamsburg. She said she remembered some things, but there were so many new features. As in 1957, she was gone after just about a day.) ⚜

Newport News *Daily Press*, August 1, 1993; and
Remembering Williamsburg—A Sentimental Journey Through Three Centuries, Dietz Press, Richmond, 1989

Queen Elizabeth II and William M. Kelso, director of archaeology for the Jamestown Rediscovery project, walk in front of the seventeenth-century tower of Jamestown Memorial Church during her brief tour. (Department of the Interior photo by Tami Heilemann)

Epilogue ❧

Jamestown Uncovered—21st Century Archaeology
By Wilford Kale

For years on Jamestown Island, the only remnant of the colonial settlement was the ruin of a brick church tower, embraced by twisting vines and encrusted by ages of sand, standing forlorn on the edge of the James River. Today, a small brick building, erected nearly 100 years ago, stands behind the tower, a symbolic attempt to replicate two seventeenth-century churches that once occupied the site.

Above ground, this was the only visible reference to the era of the settlement of the Jamestown colony. Through the last century, however, archaeologists working in the area around the tower have uncovered a vast amount of historical information that had been preserved beneath this historic plot of land.

First, there were some amateur (by modern standards) excavation efforts at Jamestown near the turn of the twentieth century, and more serious work was undertaken in the mid-1950s in association with the 1957 commemoration of the 350th anniversary of the Jamestown Settlement. Most recently, beginning in 1994, the Association for the Preservation of Virginia Antiquities (APVA), owner of the tower

An aerial view of excavations in September 1996 when archaeologists felt they had found portions of the original James Fort. (From the Associated Press via the Newport News Daily Press, *photo by Kenneth D. Lyons)*

site and more than 20 surrounding acres, launched an ambitious examination of what was believed to be the earliest occupied site on the island.

The focal point of that quest was the search for the James Fort.

For decades National Park Service personnel and others interpreting the island told visitors to Jamestown that the Fort site had been lost to the ravages of the river that relentlessly attacked the island, wave after wave and storm after storm until the U.S. Army Corps of Engineers seawall was erected in the early 1900s. By that time, it was thought that the fort already had been lost.

But Dr. William M. Kelso, who had carefully studied earlier excavation work, still believed it was possible that the fort could yet be found on the island. When the APVA decided to embark upon its project Kelso was there to provide the leadership. What was found over the course of the continuing work was nothing short of amazing.

Kelso describes these various archaeological finds in his book, *Jamestown Rediscovery, 1994–2004*, compiled and written with project curator Beverly Straube as part of a series of APVA publications designed to keep the public informed about what was being uncovered at the site

Student volunteers check a portion of a dig at the Jamestown Fort site. (From the Associated Press via the Newport News Daily Press, photo by Adrin Snider)

of America's British colonial beginnings. Kelso lamented in his volume, "So clearly the Jamestown documentary is disappointingly lean during the reign of the Virginia Company, 1607–1624. There is precious little written material about those years besides the relatively meager accounts" by George Percy, an original settler who kept a diary; Captain John Smith, whose early accounts of the settlement were in letters published as *A True Relation* in 1608 and later his *General History of Virginia, New England and the Summer Isles* (1624); and other lesser-known accounts including William Strachey's *The Historie of Travell into Virginia Britania* (1612) and Ralph

Jamie May, senior staff archaeologist for the Jamestown Rediscovery Project, works digging out at least eight intact wine bottles discovered standing on what appears to be the floor of a wine cellar under a building at the end of the James Fort. (From the Richmond Times-Dispatch, *photo by Andrew Petkofsky)*

Hamor's *A True Discourse of the Present State of Virginia* (1617), written after the authors returned to England.

Attempts to put together "the growth and development" of Jamestown through those existing documents alone, he explained in the book, "was frustrating." Archaeology and the information uncovered would be a vital way of helping to expand and enhance existing knowledge of the settlement.

Kelso explained that the primary goal of the Jamestown Rediscovery archaeological program "was to locate and uncover any remains of the first Jamestown settlement, especially traces of James Fort as it was originally constructed and how it evolved to accommodate a growing population" from settlement until the abolition of the Virginia Company in 1624.

After working for several years, Kelso and his team made THE discovery they were seeking—the James Fort. The first announcement was made in 1996, but much more work was needed to establish total credibility. By July 2003, archaeologists had uncovered the "surviving traces," Kelso wrote of the triangular fort. Only one corner had been lost to the river's ebb and flow. Part of Kelso's success was aided by the fact that little but agriculture was conducted on the island after the capital of Virginia was moved to Williamsburg in 1699. He noted that no "modern town" grew up over the original Jamestown, but farming of the land had created a plow zone of a foot or more that had to be removed before the remains of Jamestown's 1607 beginnings would be found.

Not only were thousands of artifacts uncovered dating from 1607, but the highlight element was the uncovering of circular stains in the soil that showed the upright log holes of the Fort's western wall. Finding that element clearly showed the footprint of the Fort, defining where other structures might be found. Earlier the eastern wall was found running through the site of the old tower and its revival church building.

When the 2003 findings were announced, Kelso told reporters that the goal of researchers in the future will not be to find more artifacts, but rather to find information that will enable them to determine the layout of the fort's interior and to determine how the first settlers lived.

"Knowing more about Jamestown's beginnings is like understanding your childhood. It's the key to understanding how we came to be who we are as a nation today. Our language, form of government and system of economics all have their roots at Jamestown," Kelso said.

Jeffrey L. Sheler, writing in the January 2005 issue of *Smithsonian* magazine, said that evidence uncovered during Jamestown excavations "has already caused historians to reconsider some long-held assumptions about the men and the circumstances surrounding what Yale University history professor emeritus Edmund S. Morgan once called, "the Jamestown fiasco."

Sheler quoted Morgan as acknowledging that "Archaeology is giving us a much more concrete picture of what it was like to live there." In Morgan's own 1975 history *American Slavery, American Freedom: The Ordeal of Colonial Virginia,* he argued that Jamestown's first years were disastrous. "But whether (the new discoveries turn) the Virginia Company into a success story is another question, " Morgan added.

More than 1.2 million artifacts have been uncovered in and around the fort, including items of pottery and pieces of glass. From an early well have come some Virginia Indian items-a bone needle, shell beads, glass trade beads and copper baubles-used to decorate hair and clothing.

Bly Straube, curator of Jamestown Rediscovery project, holds a wine bottle with the initials "FN" stamped on a hot glass seal that was placed onto the glass bottle. (From the **Richmond Times-Dispatch,** *photo by Katherine Callos)*

Kelso and Straube also have delighted in finding sites that conform to various known elements of Jamestown history. For example, shortly after Lord De la Warr arrived in 1610 as the new governor, he ordered the entire Jamestown site cleaned up. In the cellar of a building that was located just off the eastern wall, archaeologists found tobacco pipes, pottery shards, musket balls, coins, buttons, broken dishes, and food remains, Sheler reported.

Apparently the objects were part of that clean-up effort and date from the first three years of the colony. It is from such sites, Sheler wrote, that the Jamestown team is "revising the colony's history."

The fall and winter of 1609 was described as the "starving time," when the settlers ran out of food, could not successfully trade with the Indians, and ultimately the survivors subsisted on whatever could be found. Debris from this period has also been found in that cellar. But rather than painting the settlers as lazy and incompetent, it may be that nature was totally against the settlers, no matter their station in life.

Sheler's article makes reference to a climate study completed in 1998 that revealed a previously unknown drought in eastern Virginia from 1606 until 1612. Dennis B. Blanton, then director of the Center for Archaeological Research at the College of William and Mary, co-author of the study, explained that a study of growth rings on cypress trees in the region shows a severe stunting during these seven years. Such a drought not only would have caused the colonists problems in their efforts to grow food, but also affected the Indians who needed to raise crops for their own use. At times both Powhatan's people and the English settlers were probably vying for the same food supply, especially in the area of hunting and fishing. Strained relations occurred when the Indians could not provide settlers with the promised food assistance and hostilities broke out between them.

Additionally, Blanton, working with University of Arkansas climatologist David W. Stahle on the study, concluded that while Jamestown settlers have been criticized "for poor planning, poor support and for a startling indifference to their own subsistence," their arrival during the drought indicated

Workers in the spring of 2005 continue archaeological efforts, called Jamestown Rediscovery, at the site of the original James Fort on Jamestown Island. APVA Preservation Virginia sponsored the excavations since their beginning in 1994. (From the editor's collection, photo by Robin Hasty)

"that even the best planned and supported colony would have been extremely challenged by the climate conditions."

"I am not an environmental determinist," said Blanton in a press release. "Other factors clearly played a role in the demise of the Roanoke Island settlers and the hardships of those at Jamestown, but the droughts were certainly among the most serious problem both groups faced.

"Only multidisciplinary research could lead to such exciting discoveries as these," he added. "History, archaeology or climatology alone could not have reached these conclusions, but a combination of the disciplines enabled us to discover these significant patterns."

Kelso, in the Epilogue to *Jamestown Rediscovery, 1994-2004*, stressed that the project "is a constant interplay between the artifacts from the ground and written factual statements." From an historical archaeology perspective, Kelso said, some of the artifacts of the "first Jamestown are in many respects the 'fall out' of some of the things people did" on a daily basis … Specifically objects from pits, the moat, cellars, and a well … clearly indicate that Jamestown was a very industrious place.

"For one thing, we now know these men

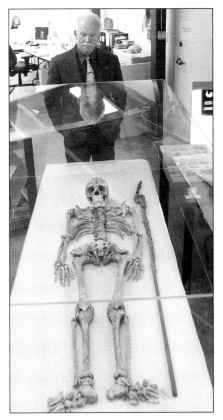

Archaeologist William M. Kelso, head of the Jamestown Rediscovery Project, stands over the "suspected" skeletal remains of Bartholomew Gosnold, captain of the Godspeed *and an early leader of the Jamestown colony. (From the* Richmond Times-Dispatch, *photo by Alexa Welch Edlund)*

first built a fort, in the amazing space of three weeks, that was never captured in battle on the most defendable high ground of the most naturally fortified piece of ground along the James River."

Kelso pointed out that Jamestown was very much different from the England that the colonists had left. Daily life was carried on, but not in the style they had known. In 1624 the Virginia Company failed, "but the Colony and the nation from which it grew, most certainly did not."

National attention was focused on Kelso's archaeological work in early May 2007, when visits by Queen Elizabeth (May 4) and U.S. President George W. Bush (May 13) were arranged in conjunction with the Jamestown 400th celebration, commemorating the settlement of Jamestown by English colonists in May 1607. Media coverage was abundant.

The queen had expressed much interest in the archaeological excavations at the

Jamestown Rediscovery project archaeologist Danny Schmidt shows an intent Queen Elizabeth some artifacts uncovered at the James Fort. William M. Kelso, director of archaeology for the project, looks on. (National Park Service photo by Mike Literst)

site of the James Fort as well and English-related artifacts uncovered there, and her visit focused on those activities. Straube, curator for the Jamestown Rediscovery project and holder of dual British and U. S. citizenships, led the queen on a tour of the archaearium, where exhibits contain artifacts uncovered over the past decade; Prince Philip, the Duke of Edinburgh toured the nearby artifacts laboratory.

After the visit, Straube recalled that the queen was interested in some "smaller finds" such as a clothing ornament of a mythical heraldry figure called the "martlet." Queen Elizabeth also was interested in a gentleman's silver "ear picker," made for scraping teeth and cleaning ears, and a seventeenth-century surgical tool, a "spatula mundane," used to treat persons suffering from constipation. The queen jokingly asked her personal physician, who was accompanying her, if he "ought to have something like that."

The royal couple then visited the excavations at nearby James Fort. On her 1957 visit the queen was told that the site of the three-sided 1607 palisade had probably been consumed by the James River. In 2007, Kelso was able to show elements of the discovered fort and a well at the fort's north bulwark that has protected artifacts in its muck for 400 years.

Kelso and fellow archaeologist Danny Schmidt showed the queen excavation trays containing chess pieces, iron knives, copper baubles and the discarded claws of crabs that had been a meal for the settlers. The queen also saw an old pipe bowl, recently unearthed. She was very interested in the work.

The Jamestown Rediscovery project goes on. New discoveries are being made and artifacts found and, in many cases, restored – piece by piece. The story of Jamestown 1607 continues to be uncovered. ⚜

Queen Elizabeth II and Vice President Richard Cheney speak with Bly Straube, curator, Jamestown Rediscovery project, during a brief tour at the Historic Jamestowne Archaearium. (White House photo by David Bohrer)

Appendix ❧

The First Settlers of Jamestown

Below are listed 92 names of those who remained in Virginia when the ships returned to England in 1607, as recorded by Captain John Smith.

Henry Adling (or Adding), gentleman
Jeremy (or Jerome) Alicock, gentleman
Captain Gabriel Archer, gentleman
John Asbie
Benjamin Beast, Gentleman
Robt. Behethland (or Betheland), gentleman
Edward Brinto, mason, soldier
Edward Brookes, gentleman
John Brookes, gentleman
Edward Browne, gentleman
James Brumfield, boy
William Bruster (or Brewster), gentleman
Andrew Buckler
John Capper
George Cassen (or Cawsen), laborer
Thomas Cassen, laborer
William Cassen, laborer
Ustis (or Eustace) Clovill, gentleman
Samuell Collier, boy
Roger Cooke, gentleman
Thomas Couper (or Cowper), barber
Richard Crofts, gentleman
William Dier (or Dye)
Richard Dixon, gentleman
John Dods, laborer, soldier
Ould Edward, laborer
Thomas Emry, carpenter
Robert Fenton, gentleman
George Flower, gentleman
Robert Ford, gentleman
Richard Frith, gentleman
Stephen Galthorpe, gentleman
William Garret, bricklayer
George Golding (or Goulding), laborer
Thomas Gore, gentleman
Anthony Gosnoll, gentleman
Captain Bartholomew Gosnoll, gentleman
Thomas Gower, gentleman
Stephen Halthrop, gentleman
Edward Harrington, gent;eman
John Herd, bricklayer
Nicholas Houlgrave, gentleman
Robert Hunt, master, preacher, gentleman
Thomas Jacob, sergeant
William Johnson, laborer
Captain George Kendall, councilor
Ellis Kingston (or Kinistone), gentleman
William Laxton, carpenter
John Laydon, laborer, carpenter
William Loue (or Love), tailor, soldier

Captain John Martin, councilor
John Martin, gentleman
George Martin, gentlamen
Francis Midwinter, gentleman
Edward Morish, gentleman, corporal
Mathew Morton, sailor
Thomas Mounslie
Thomas Mouton
Richard Mutton, boy
Nathaniel Pecock, boy, sailor, soldier
John Penington, gentleman
George Percy, master, gentleman
Dru Pickhouse (or Piggase), gentleman
Edward Pising, carpenter
Nathaniell Powell, gentleman
Jonas Profit, sailor, fisher, soldier
Captain John Ratcliff, councilor
James Read, blacksmith, soldier
John (or Jehu) Robinson, gentleman
William Rods (or Rodes), laborer
Thomas Sands, gentleman
John Short, gentleman
Richard Simons, gentleman
Nicholas Skot (or Scot), drummer
Robert Small, carpenter
William Smethes, carpenter
Captain John Smith, councilor
Francis Snarsbrough, gentleman
John Stevenson, gentleman
Thomas Studley (or Stoodie), gentleman
William Tankard, gentleman
Henry Tavin (or Tauin), laborer
Kellam Throgmorton, gentleman
Anas Todkill, soldier
William Vnger (or Unger), laborer
John Waller, gentleman
George Walker, gentleman
Thomas Webbe, gentleman
William White, laborer
William Wilkinson, surgeon
Edward Maria Wingfield, master,
  councilor, president
Thomas Wotton, gentleman, surgeon,
  a Dutchman
With diverse others, to the number of 105.

Members of the first General Assembly (House of Burgesses)

From the Governor's Council

Mr. Samuel Macock *Mr. John Rolfe* *Mr. John Pory*
Captain Nathaniel Powell *Captain Francis West* *Reverend William Wickham*

John Pory was designated secretary and speaker; *John Twine*, clerk of the General Assembly; and *Thomas Pierse*, Sergeant of Arms.

Plantations and their representatives were:

For James City
  Captain William Powell
  Ensign William Spense

For Charles City
  Samuel Sharpe
  Samuel Jordan

For the City of Henricus
  Thomas Dowse
  John Plentine

For Kiccowtan
  Captain William Tucker
  William Capp

For Martin-Brandon & Captain
John Martins Plantation
  Mr. Thomas Davis
  Mr. Robert Stacy

For Smythes Hundred
  Captain Thomas Graves
  *Mr. Walter Shelley**

For Martins Hundred (also
known as Wolstenholme)
  Mr. John Boys
  John Jackson

For Argals Guifte
  Mr. Thomas Pawlett
  Mr. Edward Gourgainy

For Flowerdieu Hundred
  Ensign Edmund Rossingham
  Mr. John Jefferson

For Captain Lawnes Plantation
  Captain Christophor Lawne
  Ensign Washer

For Captain Wardes Plantation
  Captain John Warde
  Lieutenant John Gibbes

**Died in the middle of the
meeting.*

Governors of Virginia (Under the Virginia Company of London), 1606-1624

Edward Maria Wingfield,
    President of the Council, May 14–September 10, 1607
John Ratcliffe, President of the Council September 10, 1607–July 22, 1608
Matthew Scrivener, President of the Council July 22–September 10, 1608
John Smith, President of the Council September 10, 1608–September 1609
George Percy, President of the Council September 1609–May 23, 1610
Thomas West, Lord De la Warr, Governor* 1609–1618
Sir Thomas Gates, Governor May 23-June 10, 1610
Thomas West, Governor in Virginia June 10, 1610–March 28, 1611
George Percy, Deputy Governor March 28–May 19, 1611
Sir Thomas Dale, Deputy Governor May 19–August, 1611
Sir Thomas Gates, Lieutenant Governor August 1611–March 1614
Sir Thomas Dale, Lieutenant Governor March 1614–April 1616
George Yeardley, Deputy Governor April 1616–May 15, 1617
Samuel Argall, Deputy Governor May 1617–April 1619
Sir George Yeardley, Governor April 18, 1619–November 18, 1621
Sir Francis Wyatt, Governor November 18, 1621–May 1624

* "He held title until his death, June 7, 1618; represented for most of his term by deputies"

(From A Hornbook of Virginia History, *third edition, edited by Emily J. Salmon [1983])*

Acknowledgments ✤

This project could never have been concluded without the strong support of the children of Betsy and Parke Rouse, Jr.—Shepherd and twin daughters—Sarah and Marshall. Marshall Rouse McClure designed the book and its dust cover and made the volume much, much better with her ideas and enthusiasm and Sarah Rouse Sheehan always was there to lend a hand and offer encouragement as well as contributing her skillful proofreading talents.

Wert Smith of The Dietz Press provided encouragement and support and Robert Dietz understood when deadlines were broken and materials misplaced and strongly pushed the project from the start—because he liked the idea!

Special thanks go to Peter Leers, Publisher, of Hastings House Publishers, which printed Parke Rouse's first two major books, *Virginia, The English Heritage in America* and *Planters and Pioneers, Life in Colonial Virginia*. Without Mr. Leers' permission to use important elements from those two books, published about 40 years ago, this compendium would never have gotten off the ground.

Officials of Intermet Corporation of Troy, Michigan, current owners of the Lynchburg Foundry, gave permission to use several important stories that Rouse wrote for *The Iron Worker* magazine, published by the Foundry in the 1960s.

Ernie Gates, editor of the Newport News *Daily Press*, also allowed the use of numerous articles that Rouse wrote for that newspaper as well as access to photograph files of Jamestown. His grateful assistance allowed the publication of stories that added important depth and breath to the Jamestown saga.

Thanks also go to Thomas A. Silvestri, president and publisher of the *Richmond Times-Dispatch* and William Millsaps, retired executive editor and senior vice president, for access to the paper's photographic archives and to John Clarke, library reesearcher for hours of help and invaluable assistance.

John Haskell, Associate Dean of University Libraries and Director of Manuscripts and Rare Books at the Earl Gregg Swem Library at the College of William and Mary, gave permission for the extensive use of the Parke Rouse Jr. Collection, which Betsy Rouse, his widow, gave the library following his death.

Appreciation and gratitude also goes to Debra Padgett, media relations manager, Bob Jeffrey, communications specialist, and Daniel Hawks, curator, Jamestown-Yorktown Foundation; Philip Norman, curatorial assistant, Museum of Garden History, Lambeth, London; Jeffrey Ruggles, Associate Curator for Prints and Photographs, Virginia Historical Society; David Taylor, Picture Library, National Maritime Museum, Greenwich, England; John Fisher, Librarian, Guildhall Library, London; Marianne C. Martin, visual resources editorial librarian, John D. Rockefeller, Jr. Library, Colonial Williamsburg Foundation; Mike Litterst, Colonial National Historical Park of the National Park Service; Howell Perkins, Manager, Photographic Resources, Virginia Museum of Fine Arts; and Paul Relf, St.

George's Church, Gravesend, England, who worked actively to help locate the best illustrations.

Thanks to staff members of the APVA Preservation Virginia, especially Dia Idleman, for their assistance.

Also a special thanks to Andy McNeil and Randy Owen of the Virginia Marine Resources Commission for their computing expertise and advice.

Last, but certainly not least, thanks to my wife, Kelly, and sons, Walker and Carter, for their patience and understanding when time and effort was spent on this project rather than with them. For the boys, this was always, "DaDa's book."

Wilford Kale
September, 2005

Index ❧

Pictorial references are in **bold** type)

About the Editor ✛

W ilford Kale, author and journalist, is a former bureau chief and senior writer who spent nearly 30 years in the newspaper business, the last 25 years with the Richmond *Times-Dispatch*. In April, 2007, Kale retired from the Virginia Marine Resources Commission, a state agency with headquarters in Newport News, where he served more than 13 years, the last eight as Senior Staff Adviser on the senior management team.

Kale was named Journalist of the Year in 1993 by the Virginia AgriBusiness Council and has won writing awards from the Virginia Press Association and the Council for the Advancement and Support of Education (CASE). In 1993 he and several associates at the College of William and Mary won the CASE "silver" national award for the book, *Traditions, Myths and Memories*, published on the occasion of the College's 300th anniversary.

Wilford Kale (Courtesy of Wallace H. Clark)

His initial book, *Hark Upon the Gale, an Illustrated History of William and Mary*, the first encompassing history on the College in 80 years, was published in 1985. Kale has written numerous articles for magazines and has edited *Johnny Walker, His Dreams, His Success and His Vision* and coauthored *Davis Y. Paschall: A Study in Leadership*. In 1998 he was the lead writer for the book, *Goal to Goal—100 Seasons of Football at William and Mary* and is currently working on a military history of W&M.

A native of Charlotte, North Carolina, Kale began his newspaper career in 1960 with the Charlotte (N.C.) *Observer* in the sports department. He is an alumnus of William and Mary and graduated with a degree in history from Park College in Parkville, Missouri. He is a member of Phi Alpha Theta, the history honorary fraternity; the Society of Professional Journalists, serving on the national board of directors, 1985–1990; and the Society for College Journalists, where he served as national president, 1979–1981. Currently he is a master's degree candidate in history at the University of Leicester, Leicester, England. ✛